CliffsNotes™

Great Expectations

By Debra Bailey

IN THIS BOOK

- Learn about the Life and Background of the Author
- Preview and Introduction to the Novel
- Explore themes, character development, and recurring images in the Critical Commentaries
- Examine an in-depth Character Analysis
- Acquire an understanding of the novel with Critical Essays
- Reinforce what you learn with CliffsNotes Review
- Find additional information to further your study in the CliffsNotes Resource Center and online at www.cliffsnotes.com

Wiley Publishing, Inc.

About the Author

Debra Bailey is a freelance writer and editor living in Cary, NC.

Publisher's Acknowledgments

Editorial

Project Editor: Tere Drenth
Acquisitions Editor: Gregory W. Tubach
Editorial Administrator: Michelle Hacker
Glossary Editors: The editors and staff of Webster's New World Dictionaries

Composition

Indexer: York Production Services, Inc.
Proofreader: York Production Services, Inc.
Wiley Indianapolis Composition Services

CliffsNotes™ *Great Expectations*
Published by:
Wiley Publishing, Inc.
111 River Street
Hoboken, NJ 07030
www.wiley.com

Copyright © 2000 Wiley Publishing, Inc., New York, New York
ISBN: 0-7645-8598-3
Printed in the United States of America
18 17 16
1O/QT/QX/QS/IN
Published by Wiley Publishing, Inc., New York, NY
Published simultaneously in Canada

Library of Congress Cataloging-in-Publication Data
Bailey, Debra.
    CliffsNotes Great Expectations / by Debra Bailey.
        p.   cm.
    Includes index.
    ISBN 0-7645-8598-3 (alk. paper)
    1. Dickens, Charles, 1812-1870. Great Expectations--Examinations--Study Guides.   I. Title: Great Expectations.

PR4560 .B28 2000
823'.8--dc21   00–035074
                                                          CIP

For general information on our other products and services or to obtain technical support, please contact our Customer Care Department within the U.S. at 800-762-2974, outside the U.S. at 317-572-3993, or fax 317-572-4002.

Wiley also publishes its books in a variety of electronic formats. Some content that appears in print may not be available in electronic books.

Table of Contents

How to Use This Book

This CliffsNotes study guide on Charles Dickens' Great Expectations supplements the original literary work, giving you background information about the author, an introduction to the work, a graphical character map, critical commentaries, expanded glossaries, and a comprehensive index, all for you to use as an educational tool that will allow you to better understand Great Expectations. This study guide was written with the assumption that you have read Great Expectations. Reading a literary work doesn't mean that you immediately grasp the major themes and devices used by the author; this study guide will help supplement your reading to be sure you get all you can from Charles Dickens' Great Expectations. CliffsNotes Review tests your comprehension of the original text and reinforces learning with questions and answers, practice projects, and more. For further information on Dickens and Great Expectations, check out the CliffsNotes Resource Center.

CliffsNotes provides the following icons to highlight essential elements of particular interest:

Reveals the underlying themes in the work.

Helps you to more easily relate to or discover the depth of a character.

Uncovers elements such as setting, atmosphere, mystery, passion, violence, irony, symbolism, tragedy, foreshadowing, and satire.

Enables you to appreciate the nuances of words and phrases.

Don't Miss Our Web Site

Discover classic literature as well as modern-day treasures by visiting the Cliffs-Notes Web site at www.cliffsnotes.com. You can obtain a quick download of a CliffsNotes title, purchase a title in print form, browse our catalog, or view online samples.

LIFE AND BACKGROUND OF THE AUTHOR

The following abbreviated biography of Charles Dickens is provided so that you might become more familiar with his life and the historical times that possibly influenced his writing. Read this Life and Background of the Author section and recall it when reading Dickens' *Great Expectations*, thinking of any thematic relationship between Dickens' work and his life.

Personal Background

In spite of humble beginnings, little education, and the sometimes-critical literary reviewers, Charles Dickens was loved by his public, and amassed wealth, prestige, and a large legacy of published works. He was one of the few writers to enjoy both popular acceptance and financial success while still alive. The drive for this success had its roots in his childhood.

Early and Formative Years

Charles John Huffam Dickens was born in Portsmouth, England on Friday, February 7, 1812. He was the second of eight children born to John and Elizabeth Dickens. His father, John, was the son of illiterate servants. John Dickens managed to escape a similar fate when the family his parents worked for got him a job in a navy pay office. John continued his upward climb by keeping his own lowly background a secret and courting Elizabeth Barrow, the daughter of a wealthy senior clerk who worked there. The marriage succeeded, but John's hopes for further advancement fizzled when his father-in-law was accused of embezzlement and fled the country. The loss of this financial opportunity did not slow the spending habits of John and Elizabeth, who liked the upper-class lifestyle. This problem would be their downfall as time went on.

During Charles Dickens' early years, his family moved a great deal due to his father's job and spending habits. He recalled later that the best time of his childhood was their five years in Chatham, where they moved when Dickens was five, and where life was stable and happy. Dickens loved the area, learned to read, and was sent to school.

However, his father's financial problems required a move to smaller quarters in London when Dickens was ten. Their four-room home was cramped, creditors called frequently trying to collect payments, and Dickens' parents alternated between the stress of survival and the gaiety of continuing to party. Dickens wanted to return to school but was instead sent to work at the age of twelve to help support the family.

For twelve hours a day, six days a week, Charles Dickens pasted labels to bottles of shoe polish at the rat-infested, dilapidated Warren's Blacking factory. He was ridiculed and harassed by the older, bigger workers and shamed by the stigma of working in such filthy, low-class surroundings. Intellectually frustrated, resentful of his older sister (who

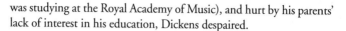

was studying at the Royal Academy of Music), and hurt by his parents' lack of interest in his education, Dickens despaired.

When his father was arrested for nonpayment of a debt, Dickens' mother and younger siblings moved into prison with his father, leaving the twelve-year-old alone on the outside to continue working. His older sister remained at the music academy. Lonely, scared, and abandoned, Dickens lived in a run-down neighborhood close to the prison so that he could visit his family. It was a firsthand experience of poverty and prison life and a reinforcement of the considerable insecurity and emotional abandonment that marked his childhood.

A small inheritance a few months later allowed his family to leave prison. Dickens was finally allowed to attend school over his mother's objections—she did not want to lose his income. School was short-lived though: At fifteen, Dickens had to return to work. Dickens never got over the time he spent at Warren's and his fierce sense of betrayal and rage at his mother's callousness stayed with him for life. Recalling that time, he said: "I never afterwards forgot, I never shall forget, I never can forget, that my mother was warm for my being sent back [to Warren's Blacking]."

Education

In the strictest sense, Dickens' formal education was limited. His mother taught him to read when he was a young boy, and his early education was of a self-taught nature. By the age of ten, he had devoured novels such as Daniel Defoe's *Robinson Crusoe*, Henry Fielding's *Tom Jones*, and Miguel Cervantes' *Don Quixote*. At nine, he experimented with writing a play for his family and called it *Misnar, the Sultan of India.*

In 1821, Dickens attended the Giles Academy in Chatham for about one year. Later, when he was twelve, he attended the Wellington House Academy in London. At fifteen, family problems required him to return to work, and so his last "schooling" was again, self-taught. He purchased a reading ticket to the British Museum at eighteen and immersed himself in its large library. He also taught himself shorthand.

Jobs

For seven years after Dickens left Wellington House, he lived at home and worked at various jobs. He spent the first two years as a law clerk. After learning shorthand he spent four years as a legal reporter, then as a shorthand reporter in Parliament. In 1834, he joined the staff of the *Morning Chronicle* as a news reporter covering elections, Parliament, and other political events. Dickens also spent some of his time involved in the theater, and he also began to write for publication. His adulthood was marked by a feverish work pace and a desire to achieve.

Love and Family

At eighteen, Dickens met Maria Beadnell, the daughter of a rich banker. She was two years older, beautiful—he fell totally in love. He wrote to her: "I never have loved and I never can love any human creature breathing but yourself." Though the relationship went well for a while, she lost interest in him after returning from finishing school in Paris. Dickens' friend and biographer, John Forster, was at first surprised that Dickens was so affected by this relationship, a pain that continued even years later. But Forster realized that this was fueled by a deep sense of social inferiority. Dickens was determined to succeed beyond everyone's wildest dreams and show them how wrong they were about him. Interestingly enough, he met Maria again years later. Eagerly looking forward to his meeting with her, and expecting the desirable vision of his youth, he was crushed when a middle-aged woman resembling his wife showed up. As his sister-in-law happily put it, Maria "had become *very* fat!"

In 1834, Dickens met Catherine Hogarth, the oldest daughter of the *Morning Chronicle's* editor, George Hogarth. Hogarth had favorably reviewed Dickens' work, *Sketches by Boz*, and the two men had become friends. Charles and Catherine were engaged in 1835 and married in 1836. It was a strange courtship: While the two held each other in affection and Catherine share his interest in a family, the courtship lacked the passion of his relationship with Beadnell. Dickens often broke dates with Catherine to meet work deadlines and sent her reprimanding letters if she protested.

As time went on, their differences grew more apparent. Catherine was not outgoing or socially poised, and she avoided the public and social events her husband attended. In addition, Catherine's younger sister, Mary, had come to live with them shortly after their marriage. Dickens was very attached to Mary and when she died suddenly in 1838 at the age of seventeen, he was devastated. His enduring grief over her death incurred his wife's jealousy. Mary, adored by Charles Dickens, would show up again and again as a character in his works.

In time, another seventeen-year-old would steal his heart. Middle-aged, hard working, and disillusioned with his marriage, Dickens met Ellen Ternan, an actress in one of his plays. She was everything his wife was not: lovely, young, and slim. Catherine, with ten pregnancies, had grown stout, and at forty-three could not compete with the younger woman. It did not take long for the marriage to dissolve, resulting in something of a scandal at the time. Catherine, rejected by her husband, left the family home. The children rarely saw her because they stayed with Dickens, and she died in 1879, nine years after he. Dickens spent the rest of his life maintaining a secret relationship with Ternan.

Literary Writing and the Rest of Life

During his early working years, Dickens had started writing short pieces or "sketches." Some were stories; others, descriptions of places in London, such as Newgate Prison or the shopping districts. One of these, "A Dinner at Poplar Walk," was published in 1833 in the *Monthly Magazine*. It was an emotional and exciting moment for the young writer even though he received no payment or credit for that first article. The magazine requested more and he started using the pen name, Boz. In 1836, he published a collection of sixty of these pieces in a book called *Sketches by Boz*. It received critical praise and sales were good. *Monthly Magazine* then asked Dickens to write a humorous novel that they would publish in twenty installments. Thus, Dickens' novel *Pickwick Papers* was born.

By the fourth installment of *Pickwick Papers*, Charles Dickens was a dramatic success. People at all levels of society loved him. The acclaim only fueled his intensity. While still working on *Pickwick Papers*, Dickens started a much darker novel, *Oliver Twist*. It was a social criticism of the exploitation of orphans both in institutions and on the streets. Not to be slowed, he began *Nicholas Nickleby* when *Oliver Twist* was only half-finished. *Nickleby* combined both the humor of his first novel with the criticism of his second, focusing on the corruption of private boarding schools.

His grief over the death of his sister-in-law, Mary, probably served as the basis for the character, Little Nell, in his next novel, *The Old Curiosity Shop*. His readers followed the story closely especially when Nell became sick—many, desperately hoping she would not die, begged the publisher to spare her. *Barnaby Rudge* was Dickens' next novel, a historical novel set in England during the French Revolution.

In 1842, Dickens and his wife traveled through America. He found himself crushed with admirers to the point of feeling oppressed by his fame. In addition, the attitudes and vanity of some of the Americans disturbed him, especially with regard to slavery, and he was frustrated by the lack of copyright protection in the States—many of his works were being published there without any payment to him. When he returned home, Dickens wrote *American Notes*. While polite, Dickens' feelings about America were nevertheless obvious. American critics were, as you may expect, hostile.

His next works were a series of five Christmas stories, of which "A Christmas Carol" was the most successful. *Martin Chuzzlewit*, a more direct attack on America and its attitudes, followed. Dickens also spent time creating and editing a newspaper, the *Daily News*, and acting in a number of amateur theater productions. At this same time, he had a number of flirtations with other women and his marriage was crumbling. Concentration and sleep suffered, so much so that his seventh novel, *Dombey and Son*, took a great deal of time and struggle to finish. However, the slower pace didn't diminish the quality of Dickens work: Philip Collins called *Dombey and Son* Dickens' "first mature masterpiece."

This period was marked by a number of painful personal experiences: the death of his older sister, Fanny, in 1848; Catherine's nervous breakdown in 1850 after the birth of their daughter Dora Annie; the 1851 death of Dora; and the death of Dickens' father, John, in 1851. Yet during this period, Dickens achieved a major turning point in his writing: *David Copperfield*. Lawrence Kappel, a modern reviewer, crystallizes the achievement:

"For the first time, he conceived a hero who could survive in the midst of the problem-filled world of experience by using his artistic imagination, like Dickens himself. This autobiographical novel was a celebration of the artist's ability to cope with the world right in the center of it, as opposed to just surviving the world by retreating to some safe place at the edge of it, as Dickens' earlier heroes had done."

The next several years would bring the publication of Dickens' next three novels—*Bleak House*, *Hard Times*, and *Little Dorrit*—as well as the anguish and personal scandal of his involvement with Ellen Ternan and his divorce from Catherine. The novels were darker than anything he had previously written and their focus was mostly social criticism: *Bleak House's* criticism targeted the legal system (it may have been the first detective novel published in English), *Hard Times* hit the government, and *Little Dorrit* aimed at the problems of society's class structure. This period also saw Dickens become involved in more theatrical productions, start a weekly magazine, *Household Words*, and give public readings of his works.

In 1859, after a dispute with the publishers of *Household Words*, Dickens left and started another magazine, *All the Year Round*. The first issue carried the first installment of his next novel, *A Tale of Two Cities*. Like *Barnaby Rudge* it was a historical novel, set in France during the riotous 1770s and 1780s. The novel was popular with his readers, but did not receive much critical acclaim. Struggling to improve the magazine's circulation and revenue, Dickens hit gold and a financial rescue with his next novel: *Great Expectations*. In spite of a mixed reception by reviewers, the reading public loved it—many proclaimed it to be his best work.

Also during this time, Dickens burned most of his letters and papers: In his success, he did not want anyone to make his life more interesting than his novels. By destroying his notes, he effectively took his insights regarding his works to the grave, leaving the interpretations of his stories up to his literary critics and readers.

After *Great Expectations*, Dickens began work on his last complete novel, *Our Mutual Friend*. It was a return to Dickens' darker style: social criticism was of a corrupt society, with London's dumps and polluted river symbolizing a modern industrial wasteland. Dickens continued to chain-smoke and overwork, maintaining a heavy public-reading schedule as well as national and international tours. From 1865 until his death, Dickens experienced a number of health problems, including a possible heart attack and a series of small strokes. The work he began in 1869, *The Mystery of Edwin Drood*, was never finished—on June 8, 1870 he suffered an apparent cerebral hemorrhage, collapsing on the floor after dinner. He died the next day.

INTRODUCTION TO THE NOVEL

The following Introduction section is provided solely as an educational tool and is not meant to replace the experience of your reading the work. Read the Introduction and A Brief Synopsis to enhance your understanding of the work and to prepare yourself for the critical thinking that should take place whenever you read any work of fiction or nonfiction. Keep the List of Characters and Character Map at hand so that as you read the original literary work, if you encounter a character about whom you're uncertain, you can refer to the List of Characters and Character Map to refresh your memory.

Introduction

Despite any literary controversy over Dickens' style, most critics agree that *Great Expectations* is his best book. The story, while set in the early part of the 1800s, was written in 1860 during the Victorian era that began with the coronation of Queen Victoria in 1837 and lasted until her death in 1901. Virtues emphasized at that time included integrity, respectability, a sense of public duty, and maintaining a close-knit family.

The period of the novel was a time of change. England was expanding worldwide and becoming a wealthy world power. The economy was changing from a mainly agricultural one to an industrial and trade-based one. With increasing technological changes came clashes with religion, and increasing social problems. Machines were making factories more productive, yet raw sewage spilled into London streets—people lived in terrible conditions as slums lined the banks of the Thames. Children as young as five were being forced to work twelve and thirteen hours a day at a poverty wage.

While the world became more democratic, so, too, did literature. Unlike the romantic literature that preceded it—literature that focused on the glories of the upper classes—Victorian literature focused on the masses. The people wanted characters, relationships, and social concerns that mattered to them, and they had the economic power to demand it. Novels were published in magazines in serial form—in ten or twenty weekly or monthly installments—and if readers didn't care for a particular story, circulation dropped and the magazine lost money. Consequently, magazines worked hard to keep their readers interested, in suspense, and buying the next copy. Dickens published *Great Expectations* in weekly installments that ran from December 1860 until August 1861.

In keeping with the desire to please readers, Dickens, on the advice of a novelist friend, changed the ending of the story from a sad one to a happy one. The different ending has been a point of controversy for readers and literary critics ever since. George Bernard Shaw felt the happy ending was an "outrage," especially because "apart from this the story is the most perfect of Dickens' works." Controversy aside, *Great Expectations*—with the happy ending—was a major success for both Dickens and his magazine.

In July 1861, *Great Expectations* was published in book form in three separate volumes, corresponding to the three stages of Pip's growth in the novel. It was published as a single-volume book in November 1862. (The chapter summaries and commentaries later in this Note give both the modern chapter numbers and the original volume and chapter numbers from the three-volume-set. The first volume had nineteen chapters while the second and third had twenty chapters each.)

The story is written as a first-person story, and most consider it a retrospective one—Pip, as an older man, telling his life's story and commenting on it along the way. However, the narrator's voice sometimes gets confusing, almost as if the younger Pip is talking. John Lucas, in his book, *The Melancholy Man: A Study of Dickens' Novels*, says: "There are essentially two points of view in *Great Expectations*. One is that of Pip who lives through the novel, the other belongs to the Pip who narrates it. And the second point of view is the authoritative one, commenting on, correcting, judging the earlier self (or selves)." Whether one or two Pips, the choice of first person is an effective one. It has a confidential, confessional quality, as if Pip is talking from his heart while sitting and drinking coffee with the reader.

The locations of the story are in London or on the marshes around Kent, near the junction of the Rivers Thames and Medway. These are areas that Dickens knew well. His happiest childhood years were spent in Chatham on the eastern coast. Nearby were marshes, the prison hulks, and convicts. Also, he lived in London for years and knew the back streets, markets, and places like Newgate Prison.

The sense of location in the novel is one of its strongest points. Dickens' imagery when describing area and place is powerful—as George Orwell suggests, his "power of evoking visual images . . . has probably never been equaled. When Dickens has once described something you see it for the rest of your life."

The story has a three-part structure similar to that of a play, which is fitting, given that Dickens was involved in the theater for many years, writing, producing, and acting in plays. The first part of the story covers Pip's childhood from the time he meets the convict in the graveyard until the time he receives his expectations; the second examines his young manhood, learning to become a gentleman and living extravagantly in London; and finally, the third part visits Pip in his adulthood, from the time he tries to help Magwitch escape until his return from Egypt at the end of the story. The three parts in this story have a moral implication as well as time and space implications. Pip's childhood is viewed as a time of innocence and goodness while living in the Garden of Eden. His young manhood is the fall from grace when he sins and must seek an end to his suffering, and his adulthood is seen as a time of redemption when he achieves forgiveness and inner peace.

The plot is complicated and twisting, full of surprises and complexities (part of the requirement of keeping magazine audiences interested from week–to-week). Dickens includes a tremendous number of and detail for his characters, and although some critical reviewers have suggested that his characters were one-dimensional, out of control, and therefore not true representations of real people, reviewer Thomas Connolly suggests that Dickens was at a high point for character development in *Great Expectations*: "Dickens had learned how to make his characters complex so that they function economically both in the basic plot and in the thematic presentation."

Other elements to be aware of include Dickens' use of humor and satire, irony, repetition to create tension, and the use of inanimate objects to convey emotion.

You can find multitudes of interpretations as to what the novel "means;" however, most reviewers place the major themes of the novel into three broad categories: moral, psychological, and social.

Moral themes include good versus evil, moral redemption from sin, wealth and its equal power to help or corrupt, personal responsibility, and the awareness and acceptance of consequences from one's choices. Psychological themes, explored through Pip's personal and moral growth, include abandonment, guilt, shame, desire, secrecy, gratitude, ambition, and obsession/emotional manipulation versus real love. Social themes that show up in the book include class structure and social rules, snobbery, child exploitation, the corruption and problems of the educational and legal systems, the need for prison reform, religious attitudes of the time, the effect of the increasing trade and industrialization on people's lives, and the Victorian work ethic (or lack thereof). With regard to work, it is interesting that the story takes place in people's "off time." Rarely is anyone ever shown working, especially the gentlemen of the story. Herbert seems to be able to take a lot of time off from work to do things with Pip. George Orwell attributes this to Dickens' Victorian view of life. A gentlemen, in Dickens' view, should strive to get a lot of money, then settle down in an ivy-covered house with servants and children all around. The desire is complete idleness except for the activities of sitting around the fire talking to friends, eating, or making more children. Cultural trends aside, the turbulence, abandonment, and insecurity of his childhood years no doubt made the theme of family hearth and home a strong one for Dickens.

An additional feature of *Great Expectations* is its autobiographical nature. H.M. Daleski, in his book on Dickens, notes that *Great Expectations* is "one of Dickens' most personal novels . . . it bears the marks of his own cravings to an unusual degree." Before writing the novel Dickens reread his autobiographical story, *David Copperfield*. While one object of this rereading was to avoid duplication in his new novel, Dickens was also reviewing his life at age forty-eight. In *David Copperfield*, Dickens focused on his own self-pity for his humble beginnings and his pride in rising above the shoe-polish factory to fame and wealth. *Great Expectations*, however, has a more mature analysis of life. Pip and Dickens undergo a humbling self-analysis that results in the wisdom that fortune does not equal personal happiness.

There are some differences between Dickens and Pip, though. While Pip never earns his fortune, Dickens did. Dickens worked intensely throughout his life while Pip rather has an aversion to working too hard. Also, Dickens loved his work, working passionately in his writing and theatrical pursuits. Pip seems fairly unemotional when describing his work with Herbert's firm—to him, it is a means to survive—and he lacks passion for anything in the novel except Estella, and even with her, his emotions are repressed, rather the antithesis of Dickens' and his fire for life.

A Brief Synopsis

Part I

Pip is an orphan living on the Kent marshes with his abusive sister and her husband, Joe Gargery, the village blacksmith. While exploring in the churchyard near the tombstones of his parents, Pip is accosted by an escaped convict. The convict scares Pip into stealing food for him, as well as a metal file to saw off the convict's leg iron. Returning with these the next morning, Pip discovers a second escaped convict, an enemy of the first one. Shortly afterward, both convicts are recaptured while fighting each other.

Pip's pompous Uncle Pumblechook arranges for Pip to go to the house of a wealthy reclusive woman, Miss Havisham, to play with her adopted daughter, Estella. The house is a strange nightmare-world. Miss

Havisham's fiancé jilted her on her wedding day and she still wears her old wedding gown, although she's now elderly and wheel-chair-bound. The house has been left as it was on her wedding day and even the old wedding cake is still on the table. Estella is beautiful but haughty and tells Pip that he is coarse and common. Pip is immediately attracted to Estella in spite of how she and Miss Havisham treat him. Although the visits are emotionally painful and demeaning, Pip continues to go there for several months to play with Estella and to wheel Miss Havisham around. He also meets her toady relatives who want her money and hate Pip. Pip does earn a kiss from Estella when he beats one of the relatives, the Pale Young Gentleman, in a fistfight. Pip tries to better himself to win Estella's admiration by working harder with his friend, Biddy, at night school. Biddy's grandmother runs the night school.

After a number of months, Miss Havisham pays for Pip's black-smithing apprenticeship with Joe. Pip had looked forward to that for years, but now that he has seen "genteel" life, he views the forge as a death sentence. However, he hides his feelings from Joe and performs his duties. During this time, he encounters a strange man at the Jolly Bargemen, a local pub. The man has the file that Pip stole for the convict years before. The man gives Pip two one-pound notes. Pip continues to visit Miss Havisham on his birthday and on one of these occasions, his leaving work early instigates a fistfight between Joe and Joe's assistant, Dolge Orlick. Orlick resents Pip and hates Pip's abusive sister. On his way home from that visit, Pip finds out his sister was almost murdered and is now mentally crippled. Biddy comes to live with them to help out. Pip is attracted to her even though she is not educated and polished like Estella.

One evening, a powerful London lawyer, Mr. Jaggers, visits Pip and Joe and informs them that Pip has "great expectations." Pip is overjoyed and assumes the windfall is from Miss Havisham, who wants to prepare him for Estella. He gets a new suit of clothes and is amazed at how differently he is treated by Mr. Trabb, the tailor, and by Uncle Pumblechook. When Pip gets Trabb's shop boy in trouble for not treating Pip with respect, he realizes how money changes things. He has a conversation with Biddy and asks her to work on "improving" Joe. Pip accuses her of being jealous of him when she suggests Joe does not need improving. By the end of the week, Pip is on his way to London to become a gentleman.

Part II

In London, Pip meets with Jaggers and his clerk, Mr. Wemmick. Wemmick brings Pip to the apartment of Herbert Pocket, who, Pip discovers, is the Pale Young Gentleman he fought at Miss Havisham's. Pip is to study with Herbert's father, Mr. Matthew Pocket, to learn how to be a gentleman. Pip and Herbert become good friends and Herbert nicknames Pip, Handel. Pip spends part of his time with Herbert and part of his time with the Pocket family. Also living at the Pocket's family home are two other "gentlemen students," Startop and Bentley Drummle. Drummle and Pip do not get along, especially later, when Drummle becomes involved with Estella.

Pip is embarrassed when Joe visits him in London with a message from Miss Havisham and cannot wait for Joe to leave. When Pip returns home to see Miss Havisham, he avoids Joe's forge. Miss Havisham informs Pip he is to accompany Estella to London where she will live with a wealthy society woman. Pip is convinced Miss Havisham intends Estella for him. In London, he spends his time visiting with Estella, spending too much money with Herbert, and joining a group of useless rich men called the Finches. He also makes friends with Jaggers' clerk, Wemmick, and realizes that the stiff legal clerk has a different, kinder personality at home. Pip also realizes that he is harming Herbert financially with their debts, and with Wemmick's help, secretly arranges to set Herbert up in business with a merchant named Clarriker.

During this time, Pip's sister dies. He returns for her funeral and is remorseful over his abandonment of Joe and Biddy. He promises he will visit more often and is angry when Biddy implies that she does not believe him.

On a stormy evening back in London, Pip's world changes dramatically with the arrival of a ragged stranger whom Pip realizes is the convict from the marshes years ago. The convict, whose name is Magwitch, had been sent to Australia and was to never return to England under penalty of death. The convict made a fortune in Australia and has risked death to return and tell Pip that he is the source of Pip's expectations. Pip is disgusted and devastated, something Magwitch, in his happiness to see his "gentleman," does not notice. Pip now knows that Miss Havisham has not been preparing him for Estella, and that with his money coming from a convict he can never have Estella. He also realizes he deserted Joe for a convict's money.

Part III

Magwitch explains to Pip that he has come to give him his full inheritance as thanks for his help on the marshes years before. He tells Pip about the other convict, a man named Compeyson. Pip later learns from Herbert that Compeyson was the same man who broke Miss Havisham's heart. Pip decides he will take no more of Magwitch's money. However, he feels responsible for the danger the man is in and will find a way to get him safely out of the country.

Pip is crushed to hear that Bentley Drummle is to marry Estella. Pip visits with her and Miss Havisham and pleads with her not to do this. He professes his deep love, which she cannot fathom, and tells her that he would be happy if she married another as long as it was not Drummle. During this conversation, Estella and Miss Havisham have an argument that shows she cannot love Miss Havisham, either. Miss Havisham realizes the depth of the damage she has done and is heartbroken.

Returning to London, Pip learns from Wemmick that Compeyson is watching Magwitch. Herbert and Pip hide Magwitch and devise an escape plan. Pip also gets an anonymous note to come to the marshes where someone has information about Magwitch. He returns home and visits Miss Havisham before going to the marshes. She begs his forgiveness and agrees to Pip's request to help fund Herbert Pocket's new business. Pip starts to leave then returns to see Miss Havisham's dress on fire. He saves her but she is very ill afterward. He goes to the marshes, where he is captured by Orlick, who intends to kill him. Rescue comes from Herbert and Startop who had followed him from London. Trabb's shop boy led them to the marshes.

They return to London and carry out their escape plan with Magwitch, but Compeyson has informed the authorities and they are caught. Compeyson and Magwitch struggle and fall into the river. Compeyson drowns and Magwitch is hurt, then imprisoned and sentenced to die. Pip by now has figured out Magwitch is Estella's father. He visits and cares for Magwitch until the man dies in prison. Afterward, Pip attends Wemmick's wedding. Pip also gets very sick and is himself arrested for not paying his debts. Joe comes and nurses Pip back to health and tells him Miss Havisham has died, leaving a large amount of money to Mr. Matthew Pocket. Before returning to his forge, Joe also pays off Pip's debt. Pip goes home, intending to make amends with Joe and marry Biddy. He arrives just in time to celebrate Joe and Biddy's wedding. Pip leaves shortly afterward for eleven years in Cairo, working with Herbert in his business. When he returns, he visits with Joe and Biddy and meets their son, little Pip. He also meets with Estella. She is a widow now after years in an abusive marriage to Drummle. She and Pip part, but the implication is that this time they will be together.

List of Characters

Marsh Area Group

Pip (Philip Pirrip, Handel) The narrator of the story who tells of his rise to wealth, his desertion of his true friends for that wealth and a chance with Estella, and his humbling by his own arrogance. At the end of the story he has learned wealth does not bring happiness.

Joe Gargery The kind blacksmith married to Pip's sister who is the moral reference point for most characters in the story. In spite of Pip's snobbery, Joe remains faithful and loving to him and is always there in Pip's hour of need.

Mrs. Joe Gargery (Georgiana M'Ria) Pip's abusive older sister who constantly reminds Pip of all she has done for him, especially "raising him up by hand." She is attacked by Orlick and later dies.

Biddy The young girl from Pip's night classes who helps with Pip's sister after the attack and later marries Joe. She is Pip's early confidant and understands him well enough to see through him.

Uncle Pumblechook Joe's pompous, self-important uncle who arranges for Pip to visit Miss Havisham's house and who arrogantly assumes himself to be the reason for Pip's good fortune.

Dolge Orlick Joe's assistant in the forge, who is responsible for the attack on Mrs. Joe and who later tries to kill Pip.

Mr. Wopsle (Mr. Waldengarver) A clerk in Pip's church who wants to be a clergyman but gives up and goes to London to be an actor.

Mr. Trabb The local tailor and undertaker.

Mr. Trabb's Boy Mr. Trabb's assistant, who ridicules Pip about his new station in life, but later helps rescue him from Orlick.

Mr. and Mrs. Hubblo Friends of Mr. and Mrs. Gargery. He is the town wheelwright, a person who builds and repairs wagon wheels.

Mr. Wopsle's Great-Aunt The old woman who holds night classes for the village children and sleeps through the classes. Biddy is her granddaughter.

Squires The proprietor of the Blue Boar, an inn in Pip's village.

Philip Pirrip, late of this parish The inscription on the tombstone of Pip's father. It is how Pip refers to his father.

Georgiana, wife of the above The inscription on the tombstone of Pip's mother. It is how he refers to his mother.

Alexander, Bartholomew, Abraham, Tobias, Roger The names on the five little "lozenges" or tombstones next to those of Pip's parents. They are Pip's deceased brothers.

Satis House Group

Miss Havisham The strange, reclusive woman who was abandoned and swindled by her fiancé on her wedding day. She has raised Estella to exact revenge on all men. Pip assumes that Miss Havisham is his benefactress.

Estella The beautiful and haughty adopted daughter of Miss Havisham who taunts and attracts Pip. She does not know she is the daughter of criminals—Molly and Magwitch. She is trained to mistreat all men but after an abusive marriage grows to be a kinder person.

Mrs. Camilla, Mr. Raymond (Cousin Raymond, Mr. Camilla), Sarah Pocket, Georgiana Pocket Miss Havisham's toady relatives who pretend to care but are waiting to inherit her money. They resent Pip and see him as a threat.

London Group

Mr. Jaggers An immensely successful London trial lawyer; feared by all but loved by none. He first tells Pip of his expectations and serves as his guardian. He was Magwitch's trial lawyer and is Miss Havisham's personal attorney.

John Wemmick The chief clerk for Jaggers. In the office, he is unemotional but at home is a caring, gentle man who becomes friends with Pip.

Molly The seemingly docile and obedient servant of Mr. Jaggers, who has powerful hands, a supposedly wild nature, and an infamous past. She is Estella's mother and only Jaggers and Wemmick know this until Pip figures it out.

Aged Parent (Aged P.) Wemmick's delightful and deaf father.

Miss Skiffins John Wemmick's lady friend and later, his wife.

Mr. Skiffins Miss Skiffins brother, who helps Pip set Herbert up in business.

Herbert Pocket (Pale Young Gentleman) Pip first meets him at Miss Havisham's when the two have a fistfight. They later live together in London and become best friends. Herbert is kind, unassuming, and loyal to Pip.

Clara Barley The gentle girl engaged to Herbert. She does not care about noble lineages and marries Herbert after her father dies.

Bill Barley (Gruffandgrim) Clara's alcoholic, abusive, bedridden father who was a former ship's purser.

Mrs. Whimple The elderly and kind landlady of the home where the Barleys live. Magwitch hides there under an assumed name.

Startop One of the young gentlemen being tutored by Mr. Pocket. He later helps rescue Pip and helps in Magwitch's unsuccessful escape attempt.

Bentley Drummle A belligerent gentleman at Mr. Pocket's who later marries Estella, beats her, and dies when thrown from a horse.

Matthew Pocket Herbert's father and Pip's tutor. He is intellectual, but ineffectual in controlling his wife or household. He is Miss Havisham's relative but is not interested in her money.

Mrs. Pocket (Belinda) Herbert's mother. She ignores her many children and spends her time tracing her noble lineage and dreaming of society life.

Sophia, Flopson, and Millers Servants and nurses at the Pockets' home.

Mrs. Brandley She hosts Estella in London and introduces her to society there.

Mrs. Coiler A busybody neighbor of the Pockets.

The Avenger (Pepper) Pip's unambitious servant boy.

Clarriker A merchant with whom Herbert goes into business.

the Jack The grimy man who does odd jobs at the inn where Pip, Herbert, and Magwitch stay during their escape trip.

Mary Anne Young maid who works for Wemmick at his home.

Convicts or Related Associates

Magwitch (Abel Magwitch, Provis, First Convict, Mr. Campbell) The convict on the marshes who later becomes wealthy in Australia and is the source of Pip's expectations. He is caught trying to escape England and dies in prison with Pip by his side. He is the father of Estella and a former partner in crime with Compeyson, who betrayed him.

Compeyson (Second Convict) A smooth-talking upper-class criminal arrested for forgery with Magwitch. Before that, he jilted Miss Havisham and swindled money from her. He is the second convict on the marshes that Pip sees—Magwitch's sworn enemy. He later betrays Magwitch to the authorities and drowns in a struggle with him.

Arthur Miss Havisham's half-brother from her father's second marriage to his cook. He is disinherited by his father and hates Miss Havisham. After his father's death, Arthur runs up gambling debts and conspires with Compeyson to swindle money from Miss Havisham and split the profits. He dies haunted by her image in his dreams.

Colonel One of Jaggers' clients in jail that Pip and Wemmick visit. He is sentenced to death and Jaggers cannot help him because the evidence against Colonel is too strong.

Sally Compeyson's wife.

Stranger at the Three Jolly Bargemen A released convict who knows Magwitch from prison and delivers the two one-pound notes to Pip in the Jolly Bargemen on behalf of Magwitch. He has the file that Pip stole for Magwitch years before, and he uses it to identify himself as Magwitch's messenger.

Character Map

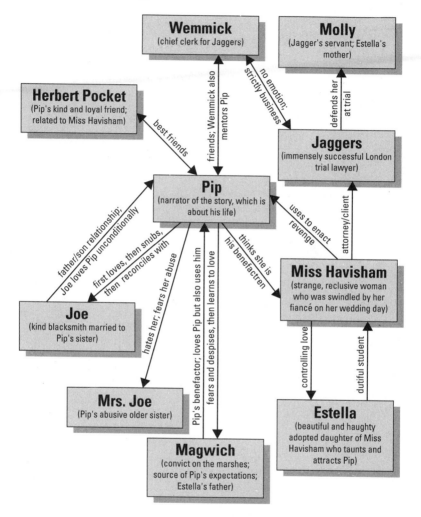

Wemmick
(chief clerk for Jaggers)

Molly
(Jagger's servant; Estella's mother)

Herbert Pocket
(Pip's kind and loyal friend; related to Miss Havisham)

Jaggers
(immensely successful London trial lawyer)

Pip
(narrator of the story, which is about his life)

Miss Havisham
(strange, reclusive woman who was swindled by her fiancé on her wedding day)

Joe
(kind blacksmith married to Pip's sister)

Mrs. Joe
(Pip's abusive older sister)

Magwich
(convict on the marshes; source of Pip's expectations; Estella's father)

Estella
(beautiful and haughty adopted daughter of Miss Havisham who taunts and attracts Pip)

best friends

friends; Wemmick also mentors Pip

no emotion; strictly business

defends her at trial

father/son relationship; Joe loves Pip unconditionally

first loves, then snubs, then reconciles with

hates her; fears her abuse

Pip's benefactor; loves Pip but also uses him

fears and despises, then learns to love

thinks she is his benefactren

uses to enact revenge

attorney/client

controlling love

dutiful student

CRITICAL COMMENTARIES

The sections that follow provide great tools for supplementing your reading of *Great Expectations*. First, in order to enhance your understanding of and enjoyment from reading, we provide quick summaries in case you have difficulty when you read the original literary work. Each summary is followed by commentary: literary devices, character analyses, themes, and so on. Keep in mind that the interpretations here are solely those of the author of this study guide and are used to jumpstart your thinking about the work. No single interpretation of a complex work like *Great Expectations* is infallible or exhaustive, and you'll likely find that you interpret portions of the work differently from the author of this study guide. Read the original work and determine your own interpretations, referring to these Notes for supplemental meanings only.

Chapters 1–3

Summary

Seven-year-old Pip walks through a churchyard on a cold, gray day before Christmas, visiting the graves of his parents. He lives in the marsh area of Kent where the River Thames meets the sea. Orphaned as a baby, he lives with his sister, Georgiana, who is twenty years older than he, and her husband, Joe Gargery, the village blacksmith. Suddenly a convict "with a great iron on his leg" confronts him. The convict has escaped from the nearby prison ships called the Hulks. After turning Pip upside down and finding only a piece of bread, the starving man threatens to eat his fat cheeks. Learning that Pip lives with a blacksmith, he agrees to let Pip live as long as he returns the next morning with some "wittles" and a file from Joe's forge. To further ensure Pip's help, the convict tells him there is a young man with him who will eat his heart and liver if he fails to return. Pip agrees to help and then watches the man stumble away.

Pip returns to his home and is warned by Joe that his sister is on a ram-page [rampage] looking for him. She returns a short time later and lets him have it on the backside with the "Tickler," a wax-tipped cane. She has "brought him up by hand," something that gains her respect from all the neighbors, and Pip notices she is quick to use the hand on him and Joe. At supper, Pip slips his bread in his pants leg to save it for the convict. Joe, concerned that Pip has swallowed the bread whole and might choke, expresses his worry. Mrs. Joe responds by pounding Joe's head against the wall and calling him a great stuck pig, then pouring Tar-water down both Pip's and Joe's throats. Later that night, they hear guns from the prison ship firing, announcing the escape of another convict.

Unable to sleep, Pip gets up early to steal the food and file, and then sets out to deliver them. He runs into a second convict and assumes him to be the young man who eats boys' livers. Running in terror, Pip finds "his" convict. While watching the man devour the food, Pip expresses concern about not leaving enough food for the young man who is waiting. The convict realizes he is not alone on the marshes, and suspecting it is an enemy of his, starts madly filing his leg iron while Pip escapes.

Commentary

Dickens gets right to the action. Within the first few paragraphs, he has introduced the main character, Pip, conveyed that the story is being told in first person by Pip when he is older, given the location of the story, revealed that Pip is an orphan with five dead brothers, and introduced the conflict: a convict in need of help. The choice of the retrospective first-person narrator is effective because the reader immediately feels part of an intimate and confessional conversation.

Description is one of Dickens' strengths *and* weaknesses, as seen in the quote describing the convict: " . . . a man who had been soaked in water, and smothered in mud, and lamed by stones, and cut by flints, and stung by nettles, and torn by briars; who limped, and shivered, and glared, and growled; and whose teeth chattered in his head as he seized me by the chin." It is rich with detail, creating a crisp vision of the man, and it is overloaded with detail, making the reader wonder if Dickens will ever stop. Yet there is no question he has a gift for bringing the reader right into the place, in this case " . . . a bleak place overgrown with nettles . . . dark flat wilderness . . . intersected with dykes and mounds and gates, with scattered cattle feeding on it."

Dickens establishes unique characters immediately, as well. Pip is "the small bundle of shivers." The convict's feelings as he stumbles through the graveyard, come across clearly: " . . . he looked in my young eyes as if he were eluding the hands of the dead people, stretching up cautiously out of their graves, to get a twist upon his ankle and pull him in." With the convict's use of w's in his words—(wittles instead of vittles) and the convict's eating style (similar to that of a large dog snapping up mouthfuls and watching for danger), Dickens defines the convict's social class, education level, current life situation, as well as his feelings about that. The description of Mrs. Gargery (Mrs. Joe) as having a heavy hand that she uses much on Pip and her husband, as well as Pip's description of his sister's method of buttering his bread and getting pins from her bib stuck in the bread, tell a great deal about her nature, how her marriage works, and what Pip thinks of her, too.

In these first three chapters, the reader also sees reoccurring character tags and repeating elements that further cement the characters in the readers' heads: Mrs. Joe constantly tells Pip about "being brought up by hand"; Joe refers to Pip as "old chap," and uses w's in words like "conwict"; the convict has an unusual clicking in his throat, and there is the recurring image of the iron shackle on his leg. (These repetitions were necessary because the story was published in weekly installments and readers may not have remembered the characters without such clues.)

The relationships are quickly established: Pip's sister rules the house, beats both her husband and brother, and is insecure and wants to be thought of as irreplaceable; while Pip views Joe, his brother-in-law, as a best friend, fellow-sufferer, and a larger species of child. The two males survive by having fun rituals such as comparing who has eaten more of his bread first and using silent signals to communicate with each other when Mrs. Joe rampages.

Pip's relationship with the convict is noteworthy. In spite of being terrorized, Pip also feels a fascination and bond with the man. He is attracted and repulsed at the same time. Instead of running away the moment the convict first turns to leave him in the graveyard, Pip stays and watches the man struggle away. This foreshadows the similar struggle in Chapter 39, when the convict returns to his life and Pip is both repulsed and concerned for his safety. There is a bond between these two. They are both—child and convict—at the mercy and control of others and as such, are both victims in life. Pip naturally responds to another "victim" and helps him, and this is the element to which the convict responds when he later rewards Pip for his kindness.

Theme

These chapters introduce several themes: right and wrong, good and evil, justice and guilt. Pip struggles with the wrong of stealing for a convict and the good of caring for a suffering human being. He also feels guilty for just being alive. From infancy, his sister has never let him forget he owes his existence to her; he is saturated with this guilt.

Dickens is careful to tie up his details, such as the threat of the young man who eats boys' livers. By having Pip discover the second convict and then remind the first one to leave enough food for the young man, Dickens introduces the conflict between the two convicts. The problem of the second convict is foreshadowed even before Pip finds him, when the guns go off the night before, announcing the second escape from the ships.

Literary Device

Humor and satire are important tools in these chapters, as well. Pip, for example, always calls his parents by the only names he knows: "Philip Pirrip, late of this parish" and "also Georgiana, wife of the above." His deceased brothers are described as "the five little stone lozenges." Even Pip's politeness to the convict, requesting to be held right-side up and expressing delight that the convict enjoys the stolen food, are funny. A bit of satire shows up when the stick used to beat Pip is referred to as the "Tickler."

Glossary

(Here and in the following sections, difficult words and phrases are explained.)

the Battery a nearby fort or gun emplacement.

gibbet a structure similar to a gallows, from which bodies of criminals already executed were hung and exposed to public scorn.

brought up by hand to spoon- or bottle-feed, rather than breast-feed.

mentally casting me and himself up Mrs. Joe tells Pip and Joe they cannot get along without her. Joe looks at himself and Pip as if adding the two of them together to see whether they would equal her.

squally troubling or disturbing.

trenchant forceful and vigorous. Mrs. Joe has a uniquely forceful way of buttering their bread.

plaister the British spelling of the word "plaster," which is a medicinal paste spread on a cloth and applied to a wound.

freemasonry a natural sympathy and understanding among persons with like experiences. Pip and Joe share the freemasonry of abuse as victims of Pip's sister. The term refers to the Freemasons, a secret fraternal society begun in the early 1700s and having among its principles brotherliness and mutual aid among its members.

Tar-water a mixture of tar and water used as a disinfectant or a nasty medicine. Mrs. Joe likes to give this generously to Pip and Joe, whether they need or deserve it.

boot-jack a device to grip a boot heel, for helping a person to pull off boots.

imbruing his hands in me Pip is worried that the young man will stain his hands with Pip's blood if Pip fails to bring the food.

copper-stick Pip has to stir the Christmas pudding and is using the stick usually used to stir the laundry, which is done in the largest copper pot in the house.

Dutch clock a cheap wooden clock that was imported from Germany.

the Hulks dismantled wooden ships no longer fit for service that are moored in British ports, such as in the marsh area of Kent, to provide extra prison space.

no getting light by easy friction In the 1820s, sulfur matches, which produced a flame when rubbed on a rough surface, were invented. This was easy friction. In this story, flames to light candles are still produced the old way by striking a flint stone with a piece of steel and igniting a splinter of wood.

Spanish-liquorice-water a sweet drink of liquorice-flavored water. There is no alcohol in it.

rimy morning a morning with frost all over anything that was damp the night before.

ague a chill or fit of shivering, often caused by malaria with its intermittent fevers.

Chapters 4–6

Summary

Mrs. Joe is busy preparing Christmas dinner and keeps pushing Pip and Joe out of her way. Pip is very tense, expecting his theft to be discovered any moment, and is relieved to accompany Joe to church. Mrs. Joe acts like a martyr because she must stay behind and prepare things. After church the guests arrive: Mr. Wopsle, the church clerk; Mr. Hubble, the wheelwright, and his wife; and Mr. Pumblechook, who is Joe's pompous, well-to-do uncle and a seed-merchant in a nearby town. Dinner is a nightmare for Pip: The table is in his chest, Pumblechook's elbow is in his eye, and he is served the scraps of food no one wants. The worst part is that all the adults constantly lecture him about being "grateful." Joe offers his meager support by giving Pip more gravy after each verbal attack. The ultimate terror though, is waiting for his sister to discover the missing food. Every time he thinks she will find it Pip clutches the table leg; when the moment passes, he releases it. Tension ebbs and flows several times until finally his sister announces it is time for the savory pie, the pie Pip gave to the convict. Pip lets go of table leg, runs in terror, and plows right into a sergeant standing in their doorway holding handcuffs.

The sergeant and his men are tracking the missing convicts and need the handcuffs repaired immediately. While Joe works on them, the astute sergeant flatters Mrs. Joe and caters to Pumblechook's ego. The pie is temporarily forgotten. Pip gets a further reprieve when Joe, Pip, and Wopsle accompany the soldiers to catch the convicts. The two are found fighting each other in a ditch. Strangely, Pip's convict risks recapture to bring other convict in. Also, noting Pip's silence, Pip's convict tells the guard that he stole some food from Joe's house. This confession saves Pip from any further suspicion about the missing food. It also provides some humorous dialogue when Pumblechook and Mrs. Joe try to figure out how the convict got into the house.

Commentary

Mrs. Joe's abusiveness and lack of warmth are evident with such comments as: "Perhaps if I warn't a blacksmith's wife, and . . . a slave with her apron never off," and her warm Christmas greeting to Pip: "And where the deuce ha' *you* been?"

Theme

Child abuse and religion were often targets of Dickens satire. The adults' attack on Pip about the young never being grateful degenerates into the ridiculous when Mr. Wopsle and Pumblechook turn a conversation about pigs into a Sunday sermon and moral lecture for the young. The satire continues as Pumblechook takes great delight in describing what a butcher would do if Pip were a pig, and then telling Pip how lucky he is to be with them.

Humor and sarcasm show in some of the holiday interactions, as well. Pip relates how Uncle Pumblechook is Joe's uncle, but Mrs. Joe appropriates him, and every Christmas when Pumblechook brings the same two bottles of wine to Mrs. Joe, she responds with the same words: "Oh Un—cle Pum—ble—chook! This IS kind!" Dickens' character descriptions are equally sarcastic: "Uncle Pumblechook: a large hard-breathing middle-aged slow man, with a mouth like a fish, dull staring eyes, and sandy hair standing upright on his head, so that he looked as if he had just been all but choked, and had that moment come to."

Literary Device

Tension is evident even in scenes where little action occurs. The scene of Christmas dinner has little action, but the back-and-forth of dialogue about pigs, church, children, and gratitude; Pip's clutching the table leg in terror every time he thinks the missing food will be discovered; Joe's serving him more gravy; and references to fugitives with iron on their legs; all work to create emotional action. It sets up the breaking point of the tension when Pip runs right into the sergeant holding the handcuffs. Similarly, the description of Joe working at the forge is a foreboding metaphor for what is going to happen to the convicts: "the bellows seemed to roar for the fugitives . . . and all the murky shadows on the wall to shake at them in menace."

Character Insight

Joe's decency of character is emphasized in these chapters. He tells Pip he would give a shilling if they "cut and run," and his reaction to hearing that the convict stole his food is simply: "God knows you're welcome to it . . . we wouldn't have you starved . . . poor miserable fellow-creatur." Joe is also aware that his station in his own house does not count for much when he observes of the food: " . . . so far as it was ever mine." It is somewhat of a mystery at this point, why a man as strong as Joe does not stand up to his wife and relatives more.

The themes of need, insecurity, abuse, secrecy, good and bad, cowardice, and guilt show up in Pip's interactions with Joe. Pip loves Joe very much, mostly because Joe lets him love him. Joe is about the only good thing in Pip's life, and at the age of seven, Pip cannot afford to lose the love of the only gentle adult around him. Therefore Pip says nothing about the food and the file he stole. Pip suffers a lot of guilt, but he prefers secrecy, emotional distance, and sacrificing the truth to losing love. Pip, the older narrator, judged himself by admitting he was a coward. These themes recur throughout the book.

There is some additional foreshadowing of the convict's later gratitude to Pip. The convict, noticing Pip's silence in front of the authorities, tells the sergeant that it was he who stole food from Joe's house. This essentially frees Pip from any blame when the missing food is discovered. The convict respects Pip's silence and help and honorably gets Pip off the hook.

Another theme in these chapters is the injustice of social classes. Pip's convict is willing to forfeit his freedom to bring the other one back. There is mention of the second convict getting easier treatment because he is a gentleman. It is obvious there is a history between these two, and their fight foreshadows darker conflicts to come between them.

Glossary

state parlour a formal parlor that is never open at any time of year except Christmas.

flowered-flounce a flounce is a wide ornamental ruffle, a cloth with pleats in it; here, the cloth has a flowered design.

Accoucheur policeman an Accoucheur was a male midwife or an obstetrical doctor. Because Pip's sister always acts as if Pip had insisted on being born, she treats him like a criminal. Pip concludes that as he were an offender at birth, he was delivered to his sister by an obstetrical policeman.

vestry a room in a church where the clergy put on their vestments and the sacred vessels are kept. Pip is scared and wants to tell someone about the convict on the marshes. One possibility he thinks of is to wait for the minister to announce the banns of marriage—that is when they announce upcoming marriages and ask if anyone has any objections—and at that moment stand up and ask for a private conference in the vestry. However because it is Christmas, no banns are announced and Pip has no opportunity for help from the Church.

corn-chandler a corn merchant.

chaise-cart a lightweight carriage with two to four wheels that is drawn by one or two horses. It sometimes has a collapsible top.

religious cross of the Ghost in Hamlet with Richard the Third Mr. Wopsle, who is a clerk in the church, says grace before they sit down to Christmas dinner. Between his desire to be a minister and thus, preach, and his love to perform in the theater, Mr. Wopsle's grace is like a religious performance of a Shakespearean play. Mr. Wopsle could be the Ghost in Hamlet or Richard III, but with a religious streak.

expectorating coughing up and spitting out.

savoury the British spelling of the word "savory," which means appetizing.

execrating cursing. When the two convicts are captured, they fight and curse each other.

whitewash a mixture of lime, whiting, size, water, and so on for whitening walls. Whiting is a chalk-like material and sizing is similar to glue. It would have been the commonly used material for painting walls in Pip's time.

Chapters 7–9

Summary

Because Pip is not old enough to be apprenticed in the forge yet, and Pip's sister has decreed that he is not to be "pompeyed" (pampered), she sends him to do odd jobs and keeps whatever he earns. He also attends the evening school run by Mr. Wopsle's great-aunt. The school is a farce—the old woman sleeps through class. Biddy, an orphan like Pip and the woman's granddaughter, gives Pip extra help with his reading, writing, and numbers. Later, Pip shows Joe a letter he wrote, and Pip realizes Joe cannot read, although Joe tries to hide that fact. Pip is somewhat patronizing and asks Joe why he never went to school.

Joe explains that his father was an alcoholic who beat him and his mother, and rarely worked. Because Joe supported the family from a young age, there was no time for school. He finishes the story by telling Pip how lonely he was after his parents died and how happy he was to have Pip's sister join him at the forge. Pip is skeptical, but Joe is firm on this, and Pip is overwhelmed with gratitude to Joe for taking him in as a baby. He feels a new level of respect for the man. The two agree that Pip can teach Joe some of the things he has learned, but Mrs. Joe is not to know. She would feel threatened by Joe's improvements, because she likes to be in charge of things.

At this point Mrs. Joe and Pumblechook return from a shopping trip with good news—Pip is to be sent to Miss Havisham's to play with her daughter. Miss Havisham is a reclusive but wealthy woman and Mrs. Joe and Pumblechook hope there will be a financial gain from this arrangement. He will spend the night at Pumblechook's and see Miss Havisham in the morning. Breakfast with Pumblechook is an unpleasant experience: The merchant barely feeds Pip while he stuffs his own face and fires math questions at Pip.

Miss Havisham is a strange woman who is dressed in an old wedding gown and tells Pip how her heart was broken and how she has not seen the sun since before he was born. Her house is the same as it was on her wedding day and all the clocks show the time her wedding was canceled. He meets Estella, Miss Havisham's proud and haughty adopted daughter, who humiliates Pip by saying he is a common laboring boy with coarse hands and thick boots. Miss Havisham tells her to break his heart, and then taunts Pip with Estella's beauty. Pip is told to return in six days, and is then brought outside to be fed like a dog. Pip is hurt and vents his fury by kicking a wall and pulling at his hair. As he wanders through a brewery on the grounds, Pip imagines he sees Miss Havisham hanging from a beam and runs in terror. Estella shoves him out the gate and sends him on his way.

His sister wants to know everything that happened and when he does not answer, pounds him on the head and shoves his face into the wall. Pumblechook comes by and adds to the pressure. Pip does not feel they will understand even if he tells them what he saw, and he does not want to expose Miss Havisham to their criticisms. Finally, he makes up lies about black coaches, cake and wine on gold plates, and waving flags and swords. Later, Pip tells Joe the story was all lies and that he feels coarse and common. Joe tells Pip lies just do not work and to think about that during his night prayers. Instead, Pip thinks about Joe's commonness and on what a memorable day it has been for him.

Commentary

Humor, satire, crisp descriptions, and tension are strong elements in these chapters. Dickens satirizes the educational system with the doddering great-aunt sleeping through her class. He criticizes child labor and the way families use their children to support them, by showing Pip's sister putting him to work and keeping the money, and then sending him to Miss Havisham's in the hope of some financial gain. (Dickens' own mother preferred him to work rather than send him to school.) He satirizes the merchant class when Pip observes that Pumblechook conducts business by watching the sadler, who watches the coachmaker, who watches the baker, who watches the grocer, who watches the watchmaker, who is working. Pip concludes that the watchmaker is the only one actually engaged in his trade. Playful humor is exercised when Pip assumes that he is always supposed to walk the same way home because his Catechism said to walk the same way all the days of his life.

Literary Device

Miss Havisham and her house are examples of Dickens' masterful use of detail and description to create character and atmosphere. Tension is present even in static scenes such as Pip and Pumblechook having breakfast. Pumblechook's firing questions interspersed with Pip's trying to eat, think, or walk gives the scene a sharp, see-sawing rhythm. The questions are almost physical attacks more than they are words.

Dickens continues to use the tool of repetition to remind his readers of a character's personality. Some examples to watch for are Joe repeatedly wiping his hand across his nose when he is in trouble with Mrs. Joe; Joe calling Mrs. Joe a "fine figure of a woman"; Pumblechook repeating his command to "be grateful to them which brought you up by hand"; Miss Havisham's finger movements and her corpse-like, wax-work, and skeleton appearance; and Pip's recurring reference to coarse hands, thick boots, and Jacks and knaves.

Guilt, gratitude, fantasy, and secrecy are themes in these chapters. Pip feels guilty when Joe describes what an ugly baby he (Pip) was, and then feels deeply grateful that Joe took him in anyway. Mrs. Joe and Pumblechook impart their good news about Miss Havisham by first reminding Pip how grateful he needs to be, and Pumblechook constantly admonishes Pip to be forever grateful to them that brought him up by hand. Secrecy is seen with Joe not wanting Mrs. Joe to know about his lessons, and Pip's willingness to lie just to keep his sister and Pumblechook from knowing the details about Miss Havisham. He feels guilty doing this, but he wants to protect Miss Havisham from the judgements his sister and Pumblechook may pass. Satis House is a fantasy world with Miss Havisham as the witch and Estella as the beautiful princess. Pip is a dreamer living in an abusive situation, so he responds strongly to a fantasy escape. He wants to keep it all to himself and does not want its glow tarnished by reality and the light of day, something his sister would bring to it. The enchantment with Satis House and its pull on Pip will intensify as the story progresses.

The themes of ambition and snobbery start to appear. When Joe compliments him for being a scholar, Pip notes that he should like to be, evidence that even at this young age he has a drive to achieve something more in life than those around him. Pip sees all the seeds in the little drawers at Pumblechook's store and wonders if they want to be free of their jails to grow. This symbolizes the themes of freedom and growth. No doubt, Pip's sister and her condescending attitude toward Joe and his work also fuel this drive. She has made it clear she does not like her station in life. Pip, in turn, shows some condescension toward Joe and his lack of education. He also describes Biddy in somewhat uncomplimentary terms, but she has knowledge and so they become friends.

Joe is a loyal man, calls his wife a fine figure of a woman and a mastermind, and when Pip tries to pick a fight with him on these counts,

Joe stops it with a fixed look and a firm word. He is also very astute and aware. Mrs. Joe likes "governing" the house and he recognizes her skills in this regard. Knowing she will be threatened if he starts to become educated, he insists on keeping his lessons with Pip a secret. Joe has the ability and compassion to recognize a person's faults and still see their good points. In spite of his father's drinking and abuse, Joe speaks of the man's good heart. Also, because of what his mother suffered with his father, Joe willingly endures Mrs. Joe's abuse so she never has to suffer the pain his mother did. Joe does regret that his choice means Pip gets hit with the Tickler from time to time. He is sorry about that and notes it as a shortcoming of his. This point will surface again in Chapter 57, when Joe speaks to Pip of his failure to protect him as much as he should have. Yet in spite of his shortcomings and lack of education, Joe is an ethical, genuine, fair man with innate goodness and a natural knowledge of life. He senses it is a problem to mix children of different social classes for play, and his morality is straight and clear. When Pip admits he feels coarse and common and that he lied in describing his visit to Miss Havisham's, Joe tells Pip that you have to be common before you can be uncommon, that no good comes of lies, and if you cannot get to be uncommon by being honest, you will never get there by being dishonest.

Pip generally views Joe as a child, though his level of respect rises after Joe's story about his parents. However, Pip also feels anger toward Joe. Pip reacts in an argumentative way to the compliments Joe pays his sister. Joe puts a quick stop to this, but Pip has an accurate sense of self here. He feels some righteous anger at the man who allows Mrs. Joe to abuse him. Pip knows that Mrs. Joe's bringing him up by hand does not give her the right to bring him up "by jerks." As with all children as they grow, Pip is also starting to realize that the all-knowing, all-powerful adults are not perfect. His anger intensifies later when Estella humiliates him over things Pip feels Joe should have known if only Joe had been more genteelly brought up. To a certain extent, Pip's later abandonment of Joe is understandable as a form of rebellion against a man that Pip feels let him down. With no way to express his passion or rage, Pip suppresses his feelings or takes them out on himself. He tries to hide his tears after Estella hurts him, resorting, instead, to kicking the brewery wall and pulling his hair out. The rising level of anger at Joe, Mrs. Joe, and Estella cannot be directed at the source, so it goes inside. This results in depression, and Pip often seems to approach life as a passive victim.

Pip's rising anger shows when he almost belligerently refuses to give his sister and Pumblechook any details about Miss Havisham. Partly, he feels he won't be understood, something he thinks is universal to children his age. He also feels attacked and cornered. Lastly, he feels protective of Miss Havisham, refusing to expose her to someone like his sister. So he lies or refuses to answer—his way of getting back at the two adults.

Character Insight

The personal interactions in these chapters between Pip, Miss Havisham, and Estella define the characters' personalities and motivations, and foreshadow a lot of the action in the novel. Miss Havisham is a hard-hearted woman who proudly wears her emotional wounds like a badge of honor. Time has no meaning for her as she has stopped all the clocks in her house at the exact time that her wedding was canceled. She does not want to know what day of the week it is and she has not seen the sun in many years. Her objective throughout the novel is to exact revenge on all men, and the first time Pip notes this is when Miss Havisham tells Estella to break his heart. He is surprised and thinks he has misunderstood her; however, as the novel progresses, he becomes very aware of what her agenda is. He does not or cannot stop trying for Estella's attention, though. In spite of the many times he will be hurt by them both, Pip is drawn to Miss Havisham's, and it is already evident, such as when he tells Miss Havisham that he wants to go home right now but does want to come back. He is hooked, admiring the unpossessable princess while she spurns him.

Glossary

Catechism a series of questions and answers children in the Church learn. When they are confirmed by the Bishop they must be able to answer these. In one part of the Catechism, the child promises to "keep God's holy will and commandments, and walk in the same all the days of my life." Pip interprets this to mean he must walk home the same way every day of his life.

Collins' Ode on the Passions Mr. Wopsle is supposed to give periodic scholastic tests to the students in his great-aunt's school to see if they are learning. Instead, he makes them listen to his performances of great orations and poems. This one is the poem, "Ode on the Passions," by William Collins (1721–1759). Collins' odes were often on nature subjects or emotions and here Mr. Wopsle plays the part of "Revenge."

fell among those thieves this is a biblical reference, referring to the unfortunate man in the parable of the Good Samaritan, Luke 10:30-35, who fell among thieves, was beaten by them, and left for dead. Pip feels that numbers and arithmetic are about as vicious to him as the thieves were to the man in the parable.

comes the Mo-gul over us a Mogul is one of the Mongolian conquerors of India and Persia. Joe uses this term to describe Mrs. Joe's heavy-handed, despotic power over them as if she were some far-eastern prince.

ablutions a washing of the body.

farinaceous containing, consisting of, or made from flour or meal. Because Pumblechook is a corn and seed merchant, his home and place of business no doubt have a fair bit of corn meal or flour dust scattered about.

gormandising a British spelling of the word "gourmandising," which here means eating or devouring like a glutton.

adamantine unyielding, firm, adamant about something. Pip adamantly refuses to answer his sister's questions when he returns from his first visit to Miss Havisham's.

plaited the right leg of my trousers as a nervous twitch, Pip sits there pleating (folding) and unpleating the cloth of his pants leg.

metaphysics speculative philosophy. The branch of philosophy that tries to explain the nature of being and reality, and the origin and structure of the universe. When Pip and Joe discuss Pip's feeling coarse and common at Miss Havisham's, Pip is speaking in abstract philosophical terms that are over Joe's head. Joe triumphs, however, by bringing the matter into simple realistic truths that even Pip concedes give him hope.

meditations prayers.

Chapters 10–12

Summary

Trying to become less coarse to impress Estella, Pip goes to Biddy for tutoring. One evening, while at the Jolly Bargemen with Joe, Pip notices a stranger who keeps watching him. When the stranger stirs his drink with a file, the same file Pip stole for the convict on the marshes, Pip knows the man has been sent by his convict and is terrified that his secret will be revealed. Instead, before the man leaves he gives Pip a new shilling wrapped in old paper. At home Pip and Joe discover the "old paper" is really two one-pound notes. Joe tries to catch up with the man but it is too late, so Mrs. Joe sets the money aside in the state parlor. Pip is haunted, both while awake and in his dreams by convicts, files, and the coarseness of such affiliations.

He meets Miss Havisham's toady relatives who pretend to care about her, and who absolutely hate Pip. They talk about a "Matthew," who is apparently an outcast in the family. Estella taunts Pip again and when he tells her she is not as insulting as the last time, she slaps him hard trying to make him cry. He tells her he will never cry for her, but knows that is a lie. While there, Pip also meets a burly man who warns him to behave himself. Miss Havisham has Pip walk her from her bedroom to the wedding-feast room that even has a large table with a rotting bug-infested bride-cake. Estella and the toady relatives join them and Pip watches as Miss Havisham amuses herself by annoying them. She dismisses them and tells Pip it is her birthday. She continues to point out Estella's beauty to Pip, then sends him to be fed outside again. While outside he meets and fights with a pale young gentleman. Estella is ecstatic over this display and even rewards Pip for winning the fight by letting him kiss her. Pip is convinced he will be arrested because of the fight, but nothing is ever said and the pale young gentleman is not there the next time Pip visits. These visits continue every alternate day for eight to ten months, with Estella's behavior varying and Miss Havisham always taunting him with her beauty. Pip tells no one but Biddy about Estella. One day Miss Havisham tells Pip to bring Joe because it is time to set up his apprenticeship. Mrs. Joe reacts with rage because she is not invited.

Commentary

"What could I become with these surroundings?" These words, spoken in the novel by the older Pip looking back on his life, foreshadow what direction his life will take and what power these surroundings and people will have over him. It is obvious to him that even if he is apprenticed to Joe, things are not going to go the way Pip and Joe dreamed they would when he was younger. Pip's enlisting of Biddy to tutor him shows his sheer determination to rise above his coarseness and shame. Already his snobbish instincts are surfacing: When he confides all his feelings to Biddy, he never notices the intense interest she has in him. She is below his aspirations so he doesn't notice her as a person, but as a tool to gain an education.

Theme

Guilt, terror, and secrecy continue to surface, both in the scene with the convict at the Jolly Bargemen, and in Pip's fear of arrest after fighting with the pale young gentleman. The number of secrets Pip is carrying within him is increasing. The theft of food for the convict years ago continues to haunt him, especially when the man with the file shows up in the Bargemen. Pip can never seem to escape the taint of the criminal element. He has never told Joe about the convict and currently has told Joe nothing of Miss Havisham or his fight with the young man there. Secrecy rules.

Style & Language

Dickens works his satire of parasitic relatives through the characters of Miss Sarah Pocket, Camilla and Mr. Raymond, and Georgiana. It is particularly telling that Dickens often calls Raymond "Mr. Camilla," mocking him as a henpecked husband at the mercy of his wife. While the relatives pretend excessive concern and worry for Miss Havisham, none of them can stand each other and Miss Havisham has one of her more normal delights in taunting all of them. They are essentially vultures waiting for her to die so they can collect her money. Dickens' descriptions are superb in adding to their distasteful personalities. He paints Sarah Pocket as "a little dry brown corrugated old woman, with a small face that might have been made of walnut-shells, and a large mouth like a cat's without the whiskers." Sarah's character tag becomes the walnut-shell countenance; the phrase repeats throughout the book.

Mrs. Joe feels threatened when Joe is summoned to Satis House without her. Her insecurity and upset at the loss of control is evident in her angry house-cleaning that night. Mrs. Joe derives her power from knowing every detail of the world around her, running everything, and reinforcing to Joe that he could never survive without her. She does this because she fears abandonment and being alone again as she was before Joe married her. If Joe handles his visit to Miss Havisham without her, Mrs. Joe fears he will think he can handle the rest of their life without her. She becomes fierce and angry because her dominance, and hence, her security, is threatened.

The dynamic between Pip and Estella that will operate for most of the novel is firmed up in these chapters. She humiliates him and tries to make him cry. He refuses to give her that power even though she makes him cry on the inside. The interesting element is her enthusiastic response when he bests the pale young gentleman in a fistfight. She is flushed with delight and lets him kiss her. There is a streak of the wild in her, and for all her calm indifference, violent emotions touch something within her.

Miss Havisham continues to operate from her agenda of revenge, though there are moments such as when Pip sings the song, "Old Clem," that she seems to enjoy him. She seems upset when she realizes one day that Pip is getting too old for play. Her willingness to reward Pip with his apprenticeship to Joe is puzzling and one has to wonder if it was meant as a reward or a death sentence. Now that Pip is obsessed with the beautiful Estella, apprenticing him in an occupation that will only make him more coarse seems to be the ultimate revenge, especially when Pip has already expressed a desire for education.

Other elements seen before continue here. Pip's repressed anger flares when he dreams of pulling the linchpin out of Pumblechook's chaise-cart, and he rages inside whenever Pumblechook rumples his hair. The hair-rumpling tag will be repeated through the book. Gratitude for being brought up by hand, the fantasy element with Miss Havisham as the Witch of the place, Miss Havisham's finger movements, waxwork appearance, and not wanting to know about days of the week, all continue as well.

Some new elements are introduced, including the large burly man with the soap-scented hands who bites his forefinger, and the description of the wedding cake with the references to black fungus, cobwebs, spiders, and beetles. The soap-scented man will surface again shortly in the novel and it is a character tag to watch for. Pip's comment that he was unaware that the man would be important to him foreshadows the role the man will soon play in his life. The spider and web references will continue through the book, especially in relation to Bentley Drummle. Also, spiders and the webs they weave to draw in and control their victims, serve as a metaphor throughout the story for the hold Satis House and its occupants have on Pip.

Some social commentaries are evident. Just as Dickens' mother wanted him to keep working to bring in money—the greed of parents who benefit at their children's expense—Mrs. Joe is hoping to reap some financial gain from Pip's stay with Miss Havisham. Dickens notes the different behaviors of the social classes when Pip decides the burly man on the stairs at Miss Havisham's is not a doctor because a doctor would have had a "quieter and more persuasive manner." The burly man's comment about having experience with boys and that they are a bad set of fellows conveys a view in society that children are not to be valued or cherished, but punished and controlled.

Glossary

one low-spirited dip-candle and no snuffers dip candles were cheap, quickly burning candles that smoked a lot from the long-burned wick they left. To avoid the smoke, the wicks needed to be trimmed with a special tool called *snuffers*. Pip indicates that it is hard to study at Mr. Wopsle's great-aunt's school even if you want to because the room is lit by only one of these candles, making a book hard to read.

public-house an inn or tavern. In Pip's time these were the hotels and restaurants for travelers.

ophthalmic steps ophthalmic means having to do with the eye in some way. The stranger in the Jolly Bargemen eyes Pip very closely and for some time. Pip does not recall anyone ever taking such ophthalmic steps with him, in other words, eyeing him so closely, before.

two One-Pound notes one-pound notes went out of circulation in England in 1821 because they were so easily and so often forged. This piece of information sets the timing for this part of the novel before 1821. It is also interesting because later in the novel the reader learns that Compeyson and Magwitch were arrested for forgery, though Dickens never confirms if they forged these notes.

pervade to pass through or spread through.

toady fawning, overly interested and obedient to someone to the point of being obviously a liar and actually uncaring.

ginger and sal volatile this was a form of smelling salts used then especially to revive ladies who passed out or became hysterical. It was a mixture of ammonium carbonate scented with dried ginger. This is used much by Raymond to calm Miss Camilla during the night when she gets so "nervous" worrying about relatives like Miss Havisham.

myrmidons of Justice this is a reference to Homer's *Iliad*. The Myrmidons were followers of Achilles. Here Pip simply means "policemen." He is afraid he will be arrested for fighting with the pale young gentleman at Miss Havisham's.

garden-mould dirt, soil, earth.

Old Clem an early Pope, St. Clement (who died around the year 100), who was patron saint of blacksmiths. Blacksmiths sang this song about him.

Chapters 13–15

Summary

To bolster her self-esteem, Mrs. Joe announces that when Joe and Pip visit Miss Havisham, she will accompany them and wait at Pumblechook's. She marches proudly ahead and carries a number of her treasured items with her as if on parade. Joe looks ridiculous in his suit, and he is obviously uncomfortable while at Satis House as he fidgets with his hat and refuses to answer Miss Havisham directly. He answers only by speaking to Pip. Pip is very embarrassed by Joe's appearance and conduct, especially when he sees Estella laughing at him. Miss Havisham gives a generous premium to Joe for Pip's service saying Pip has been a good boy.

An amazed Joe brings the premium of twenty-five pounds back to Pumblechook's and hands it over to Mrs. Joe. He is smart enough to say Pip received nothing but that Miss Havisham sends her regards and this money to Mrs. Joe. This soothes Mrs. Joe's mood. They are all shocked at amount of money and Pumblechook immediately takes them to the Court to have Pip bound, hauling Pip along so that others think he is a criminal. Later they go out to dinner and celebrate with the Hubbles and Mr. Wopsle, but Pip is tired and morose. He no longer wants to work in the forge.

Pip fulfills his obligations but he is unhappy. It is endless drudgery and he fears Estella will see him in the forge with blackened face and hands, doing his coarse work. As he is too old for evening school, he now teaches himself from books and tries to teach Joe as well so as not to be so ashamed of the man.

One day, Pip talks of going to visit Miss Havisham. Joe points out that it is a bad idea, but finally gives Pip a holiday to do it. Orlick, a journeyman in the forge who is jealous of Pip, also asks for time off. Mrs. Joe protests it all and gets into an argument with Orlick that eventually requires that Joe fight Orlick to defend his wife's honor. Joe bests Orlick and the two make amends over a beer. Pip's visit to Miss Havisham is a disaster. She tells him Estella is in Paris, taunts him about losing her, and dismisses him with the request that he return on his birthdays. After hearing Wopsle perform a George Barnwell tragedy at Pumblechook's, Pip and Wopsle walk home. They run into Orlick, who has been lurking in the shadows. Hearing that someone is hurt at Pip's house, they rush there to find Pip's sister near death after being hit on head. She will never again be on the rampage.

Commentary

Theme

Relationship themes intensify in these chapters. Between Joe, Orlick, Pip, and Mrs. Joe, the dynamics are black and ominous. Orlick resents Pip. Pip fears Orlick. Mrs. Joe hates Orlick and claims to be more than a match for him. Orlick retorts with the foreshadowing comment that if she were his wife he would drown her under the water pump. Goaded by his enraged wife, Joe is forced into a fight with Orlick to defend her honor. Afterward, the two men quietly share a beer. It is evident that the fight is not between the two men, but is a reflection of the hostility that Mrs. Joe carries within her. The whole situation has a murderous tone to it and is at a flash point.

Mrs. Joe displays her insecurity and fear when she is left out of dealings with Miss Havisham. She pouts all night while cleaning, and makes a self-important display of herself and her treasures as she walks to Pumblechook's. Her reaction to Miss Havisham's money indicates her concern for wealth and disregard of Pip's happiness. Mrs. Joe's raging at Orlick and their taunts back and forth foreshadow the harm to come. She is demeaning and bent on controlling everyone. Orlick, a deprived member of society, already feels jealous of Pip and has little self-esteem—Mrs. Joe's insults make him feel even worse and trigger a violent reaction. Orlick is just unstable enough to actually act out his rage, doing to Mrs. Joe what everyone else would like to do—kill her.

Character Insight

Joe's ignorance and wisdom are both evident. He is uneducated and cannot spell even simple words like "out." When he wants to let people know the forge is closed he writes "hout." Yet Joe has a natural wisdom and dignity about relationships. He is happy to learn things from Pip, but he is content with who he is in life. He is honorable and so defends his wife, makes amends with his co-worker, and stands his ground at Miss Havisham's when he says that Pip's happiness, not money, is what matters most. When Pip wants to visit Miss Havisham, Joe tells him she might view this as seeking something more from her when she has indicated the relationship is over. When Pip persists, saying he wants to thank her, Joe, speaking in the symbols of his trade—door-chains, gridirons, and brass—tries to explain that there is no gift Pip could offer her in thanks that she does not already have. Joe intuitively knows the visit is a mistake, yet he does not stand in Pip's way and merely tells him that this visit should be the last unless Miss Havisham encourages more.

Pip, on the other hand, lacks Joe's intuitive and natural dignity and knowledge. When they meet with Miss Havisham, Pip is embarrassed by Joe. The older Pip who is narrating the story says, "I am afraid I was ashamed of the dear good fellow—I *know* I was ashamed of him." Interestingly, Miss Havisham shines here. "Miss Havisham . . . understood what he really was, better than I." She grasps Joe's dignity and honesty, treats him with respect, and does not mock him. But Pip, ashamed of his home, feels trapped in the forge. He recognizes that Joe has always brought a sanctity to their home, but having had a taste of Satis House, Pip can never be happy in the forge. As to whose fault this is, Pip, the narrator, does acknowledge that some was his, some was his sister's, and some was Miss Havisham's.

Literary Device

Pumblechook continues to be ridiculous by pompously pretending he knew about the money Miss Havisham gives to Joe, and acting as if he were responsible for this. Also, themes of guilt and crime continue. Pip feels tremendous guilt about not wanting to work in the forge. He is also mortified when Pumblechook drags him to court to be apprenticed, because everyone thinks he is a common criminal. Some character tags and symbols that appear in these chapters: Joe playing with his hat at Miss Havisham's, which will appear again later in Chapter 27, when Joe visits Pip in his "gentleman's" flat; the white-sailed vessels going out to sea, symbolizing Miss Havisham and Estella and the sense of freedom and excitement Pip feels around them. Mrs. Joe's "rampage" tag is used to show that her role in the story is almost over, when Pip says she will never again be on the rampage.

Glossary

Great Seal of England in plaited straw the Great Seal of England is an important symbol carried by the Lord Chancellor. Here, Mrs. Joe carries her plaited-straw basket importantly, like her own straw version of the Great Seal of England.

a pair of pattens protective footgear for wet weather. They were wooden soles strapped on over the shoes.

Rantipole Mrs. Joe sarcastically calls Pip this name and the reference has a couple possible meanings. There were two references in Dickens' time—one referred to a wicked child in a children's story of the time, the other to Napoleon III, who was much in the news in 1860 waging wars and generally disturbing things in Europe. In either case, the name is not a compliment.

fired a rick set fire to a haystack. Pip's reference to this crime means people would have viewed him as a major criminal because at that time, children even as young as seven were sometimes hanged for arson.

a tract ornamented with a woodcut a tract was a pamphlet expounding on some topic, usually religious or political. Pictures were often applied by cutting a design into a block of wood, inking the wood, and then pressing it onto the paper.

excrescence an ugly, abnormal, or disfiguring addition to something. At his party for his apprenticeship, Pip is miserable while the adults are having a great time. Thus, Pip is an excrescence on their fun.

The Commercials underneath . . . Tumbler's Arms When Mr. Wopsle does his "Ode on the Passions" performance at Pip's party, he throws his "sword down in thunder," making so much noise that the traveling salesmen in the rooms below complain. The waiter is telling Mr. Wopsle that the inn is not a place for circus performers as the Tumbler's Arms is, so quiet down.

O Lady Fair a popular song of the time, written and set to music by the Irish poet Thomas Moore (1779–1852).

descrying to discern, or think you see, something.

shark-headed screws round-headed screws.

gridiron   a framework of metal bars or wires on which to broil meat or fish. Joe is trying to use terms of his work to tell Pip there is nothing special he could make and bring to Miss Havisham that would be enough even if he were the best of craftsmen. Even the best cannot change a gridiron into something special.

Cain or the Wandering Jew   Pip describes Orlick as a skulking, evil sort of person. He associates Orlick's appearance and mannerisms with the Bible character Cain, a fugitive and vagabond after killing his brother Abel, and with the Wandering Jew, a legendary medieval character who wandered the earth as punishment for his cruelty to Christ.

sluice-keeper   sluices were floodgates that controlled the flow of water through the marshes. The sluice-keeper was responsible for managing these gates. Orlick lodges with the sluice-keeper near the forge.

George Barnwell; meditating aloud in his garden at Camberwell; died amiably at Camberwell; game on Bosworth Field; and in the greatest agonies at Glastonbury   after Pip visits Miss Havisham, he stops at Pumblechook's and listens to Wopsle perform the part of an uncle who is murdered in the play *The London Merchant*. Barnwell is the young hero in the story who kills the uncle. As Pip and Wopsle walk home from Pumblechook's, Wopsle continues his rendition of famous death scenes: the Camberwell reference is still from the Barnwell tragedy, and the Bosworth Field reference is from *Richard III*; the Glastonbury reference is unclear because Dickens may have confused Glastonbury with Swinstead Abbey, from Shakespeare's play *King John*.

Chapters 16 and 17

Summary

The police investigation into the attack on Mrs. Joe is a comedy of errors and false accusations. The investigators leave without solving the crime. The only things known for sure are that the candle in the room was blown out and she was hit on the back of the head with a rusted convict's leg iron while she faced the fireplace. Joe and Pip have alibis, and Orlick seems to. She has survived but now requires constant care. Biddy, whose grandmother has died, comes to take care of her and it is Biddy who learns to understand the woman's signals, particularly the letter "T" she keeps writing. Biddy determines it is really a hammer and Mrs. Joe is asking for Orlick, who Mrs. Joe now seems very anxious to please.

Pip has become vain as his self-education progresses. He observes that Biddy is common and not very beautiful, though she is pleasant, wholesome, and sweet-tempered. In his arrogance about his own progress he manages to insult hers; even his attempts to compliment her are patronizing and condescending. He tells her he wants to become a gentleman to win Estella. Biddy tries to point out that given Estella's treatment of him, she may not be worth having. He agrees, but further insults Biddy by telling her that he wonders why he cannot love her instead. She quickly understands where things stand and responds that a relationship between she and Pip would not work. Orlick, who has been following them as they talk, has been making advances to Biddy that she fears and does not want. Pip is jealous and judgmental, and does his best to frustrate Orlick's overtures.

Commentary

Theme

Ambition, snobbery, obsession, secrecy, guilt, and shame are undercurrents here. Like Dickens, who taught himself with books from the library, Pip tries desperately to become educated and less coarse by teaching himself. Yet there is no escape from his prison, the forge, and Pip feels guilty that he hates the forge so much. Ambition can be a good force unless the motive is only to please another—Pip knows in his heart that pursuing Estella is wrong but he cannot let go. Biddy tries to get Pip to understand that striving to please a woman who despises you is a mistake, but she astutely sees it is a lesson that the "student" cannot learn.

Character Insight

Pip has become a snob, so wrapped up in himself and Estella that he fails to see the wonderful person Biddy is. For all his book-learning, he is ignorant in human relationships. He repeatedly puts Biddy down such as when he is surprised at her level of knowledge. Biddy gracefully stands up for herself, yet she is hurt and quickly knows the score. She remains kind but tells Pip they will never be together, something that annoys him. Pip wants everything. He wants Estella, but wishes he could love Biddy. He does not care about Biddy, but does not want her to reject him. He is jealous of the attention Orlick pays her, so he tells her he would not think much of her if she encouraged him. And he is not smart enough to realize he has no right to judge or dictate anything to her. Pip is a mess. He does, however, have moments of insight, such as when he comments that he "felt vaguely convinced that I was very much ill used by somebody, or by everybody." He is being used, even if at a distance, by Miss Havisham, Estella, Mrs. Joe, and Pumblechook. His true self realizes that something is wrong, but he just cannot see it yet.

When he discovers that the weapon his sister was attacked with is probably the same leg iron his convict filed off years ago, he feels much guilt. Old secrets and sins seem to multiply the evil they do and those sins, along with the taint of criminal associations, continue to haunt him. Joe continues to show his fineness when he looks on his wounded wife with moist eyes and comments that she was a "fine figure of a woman." Orlick's guilt is implied by the hammer Mrs. Joe draws and by her desire to please him; however no one makes the connection.

Glossary

the Bow-street men from London; extinct red waistcoated police there were two groups—the Bow Street Runners and the Bow Street Patrol. The latter wore red uniforms, worked as patrols in London, and were often confused with the former. The Runners were plainclothes detectives in London who often went out into the provinces to investigate serious crimes.

stile a step or set of steps used in climbing over a fence or wall. Another definition is a turnstile or post with revolving horizontal bars, placed in an entrance to allow the passage of persons but not of horses, cattle, and so on. Pip and Biddy are walking on the marshes near the sluice-gate, which is a gate that controls the flow of water onto the marshes. Either definition—a turnstile or a wall with steps climbing over the wall—works here because either one may be used to prevent animals and unaware persons from getting hurt near the sluice-gate.

supposititious case hypothetical case.

Chapters 18 and 19

Summary

Pip, in his fourth year of apprenticeship, joins Joe at the Jolly Barge-men, where they listen to Wopsle expound on a criminal story in the newspaper. A strange man takes issue with Wopsle's comments and proceeds to destroy his arguments. The man repeatedly bites his forefinger and throws his forefinger toward Wopsle as he makes his points. Pip recognizes him as the soap-scented man from Miss Havisham's. The man asks to speak to Joe and Pip, so they return home and sit in the state parlor. He tells them his name is Jaggers, and he is a lawyer from London with news for Pip. The young man is to come into a handsome property and therefore has great expectations. Joe and Pip are both astounded. Pip views this as his dream come true, and Pip thinks it is Miss Havisham's doing because this man is her lawyer. The two conditions to his expectations are that he must keep the name of Pip and not ask the name of his benefactor. That person will step forward when the time is right. Jaggers mentions that Pip should study with someone to learn to be a gentleman and mentions Matthew Pocket, a relative of Miss Havisham's. Jaggers is clear that he makes no recommendations, but merely gives the information. He further states that, in this matter, he is paid or he would not be there, and if his opinion were asked, he would not have recommended this gift. When Jaggers badgers Joe about financial compensation for losing Pip in the forge, Joe is insulted and is ready to fight Jaggers.

Joe struggles to control his sadness that evening, and Pip is angry with him for being sad. Yet Pip also gets angry when Joe and Biddy manage to show genuine happiness for him and ask about his preparations. When Pip heads to town to get a new suit of clothes he observes that even the cows in the pasture seem to view him more respectfully. Trabb, the tailor, cannot be helpful enough and yells at his assistant for not being respectful enough to Pip. Even Pumblechook falls all over Pip. The pompous man shakes his hand, feeds him, and pretends that they were great friends when Pip was a child.

Pip speaks to Biddy about trying to work with Joe to be less backward in his learning and manners so he will be ready when Pip "elevates" him. Biddy observes that perhaps Joe is aware of what he is and is happy and dignified filling that role with respect. Pip gets angry, accusing her of jealousy, and remarks that he will not ask anything more of her. She apologizes if she has given any slight and notes that whatever he feels toward her, it will not change what she feels for him. She does observe though that "a gentleman should not be unjust neither."

Before leaving, Pip wears his clothes to Miss Havisham's where he succeeds in making Sarah Pocket jealous. Miss Havisham feeds his belief that she is his fairy godmother. On the day of his departure, Pip asks to leave alone, not wanting to be seen with Joe and Biddy when he greets the stage in his new clothes. He tries to be indifferent about leaving, but cries as he walks away. On the coach, he struggles with mixed feelings about the way he left and considers getting off the coach and returning to make amends. However, he cannot decide, and after a bit, the coach has gone too far to go back.

Commentary

Description, repetition, and tags abound. Jaggers' tags include his watch chain, bushy eyebrows, the black dots of his beard, and his habit of biting his forefinger. He repeats his instructions that he deals only in facts, makes no recommendations, and wants everyone clear on what to expect and not expect from him. Jaggers is an honest and up-front man. He is not a warm person, but he is a much more honorable one than Mrs. Joe ever was with her emotional games and blackmail. Other tags are Pumblechook's "May I?" every time he shakes Pip's hand, and Sarah Pocket's walnut-shell countenance, which in her jealousy of Pip has now gone from brown to green and yellow.

Joe's emotional depth is beautifully revealed in these chapters. "Joe laid his hand upon my shoulder with the touch of a woman. I have often thought of him since, like the steam-hammer, that can crush a man or pat an eggshell, in his combination of strength with gentleness." Joe is comfortable with both sides of his emotions and he is clear about his priorities in life. The man's heart is breaking at losing Pip: Dickens shows this when Joe scoops his eyes trying not to cry and silently grips his knees as he sits in front of the fire struggling to control his emotions. His fierce love for Pip is seen when he is ready to take Jaggers apart for insinuating that any amount of money could ever replace Pip. Yet the gentleness returns immediately when Pip takes him aside to calm him.

It is unclear who wins the prize for boorishness in these chapters: Pip or Pumblechook. The connection between these two is that at least for part of the book, they are very much alike. Pip, in coming into property, becomes just like Pumblechook. Pumblchook falls all over Pip, constantly asking "May I" and trying to shake his hand. He feeds him, offers to take care of Joseph in his "deficiency," and twists the memories of Pip's childhood to represent himself as sporting with the infant Pip and playing their "boyish games of sums." Pumblechook even remarks of Mrs. Joe, "let us never be blind to her faults of temper," in his attempts to ingratiate himself to Pip. He also suggests that investing capital in his business would be welcomed especially because, as he reminds Pip, he is "the humble instrument of leading up to this." Pumblechook never misses a moment to take the credit for something and the way he treats someone changes with their financial status. This foreshadows a similar change when Pip is a gentleman.

Pip observes how money changes things: how much nicer Mr. Trabb, the tailor, treats him and how much trouble Trabb's boy gets into when he is not respectful enough to Pip. At home, Pip's behavior is pompous and snobbish. While he has moments of sadness, for example, when he feels he will miss his room, he spends his time being peevish to Biddy and Joe. Pip is irritable when they are sad at his leaving, and he is irritable when they are happy for his good fortune. There is no pleasing him. He is condescending to Biddy in his desire to improve Joe and cannot understand that Joe is worthy of respect. Biddy's response to him, while appropriate, merely infuriates Pip. He is projecting onto them his own base behaviors, and instead of seeing how badly he is acting, he convinces himself they are the ones who are jealous and behaving badly. Biddy shows true dignity, restraint, and compassion when she kindly defends Joe, apologizes to Pip, and tells Pip her feelings toward him will always be the same. In a brilliant yet subtle way, however, she lets him know that he is wrong and that even though he is a gentleman, he has no right to misjudge people and treat them badly. Pip is almost sickening when he magnanimously "forgives" Biddy. The extent of his delusions is apparent when he thinks that even the cattle in the field view him with a new level of respect. The struggle between good and evil in him is evident in the moments when Pip has second thoughts about his behavior, such as when he ponders getting out of the coach and going home to say a better good-bye. However the shallowness of his character at this point in his life wins out. Waiting until it is too late to go back, he shrugs off personal responsibility and "overcomes" his moment of goodness.

Glossary

Timon of Athens and Coriolanus two of Shakespeare's plays. The hero of the first is known for speaking abusively and the hero of the second, the beadle, is known for arrogance.

settle a long wooden bench with a back and armrests.

subterfuge any plan, action, or device used to hide one's true objective or evade a difficult or unpleasant situation. When Jaggers discounts Wopsle's conclusions about a murder Wopsle is discussing, the rest of the people listening start to question whether Wopsle has an ulterior motive in drawing the conclusions he has.

Brag is a good dog, but Holdfast is a better a proverb meaning that silence is better than boasting.

expostulatory having to do with an earnest objecting.

obtruded offered or forced upon others unasked.

the rich man and the kingdom of Heaven Pip is uncomfortable because the clergyman in church reads this Bible passage right after Pip finds out he has come into wealth. The Bible reference is Matthew 19:24: "It is easier for a camel to go through the eye of a needle, than for a rich man to enter into the kingdom of God."

the change come so oncommon plump a change coming so suddenly and all at once. Joe is commenting on how the news of Pip's expectations just caught him off guard at first, but after a night's sleep he is dealing better with it.

collation a light meal.

apostrophising the fowl the British spelling of the word "apostrophizing," which means the addressing of someone or something, as in a speech or play. Pumblechook is speaking to the chicken that he is about to eat, about Pip's good fortune.

hand-portmanteau a traveling case or bag.

Chapters 20–22
(Volume II, Chapters 1–3)

Summary

Pip arrives at Jaggers' office, located in a rundown business area of London. The lawyer is not there, so Pip waits in his office, a dark, dismal, airless room accented with odd things like an old rusty pistol, a sword in a scabbard, and two casts of swollen faces. Jaggers chair reminds Pip of a coffin. Unable to take the oppressiveness, Pip walks around the area, passing through the filth, fat, and foam of the Smithfield markets. He walks near Newgate Prison where a drunk minister of justice shows him the gallows, and into Bartholomew Close where many people are anxiously waiting for Jaggers. They hope to hire him or hear news of relatives' cases. Jaggers arrives and is condescending to all of them, dealing only with those who have paid their bills. Speaking to witnesses in his office he is careful not to hear, do, or say anything illegal, staying just within the law in all his dealings.

Pip learns from Jaggers that he will be staying at Barnard Inn with Mr. Pocket's son until Monday, when they will go to Mr. Pocket's house. Pip is given an allowance and Jaggers tells him frankly that he will track Pip's spending to know when Pip is running up debts. He fully expects Pip will do this. His clerk, Wemmick, a dry man who wears many mourning rings from dead clients, takes him to Barnard Inn. The inn is dismal and dreary, and because of his surroundings, Pip feels that London is overrated. He meets Herbert Pocket, whom Pip realizes is the pale young gentlemanfrom Miss Havisham's. The two become good friends and Herbert nicknames Pip, Handel, after a piece of Handel's music, the *Harmonious Blacksmith*. Over dinner, in between gently correcting Pip's table manners, Herbert tells Pip about Jaggers, Miss Havisham, Estella, Herbert's father, and himself.

Pip's guardian, Jaggers, is also Miss Havisham's lawyer. He is acquainted with Herbert's father, Matthew Pocket, because Matthew is Miss Havisham's cousin, though the two are not on good terms. Herbert explains that Miss Havisham was to be married to a fine gentleman who swindled some money from her, and then left her at the altar.

The man apparently conspired with Miss Havisham's half-brother, Arthur, who was in debt and did not like Miss Havisham. As to Estella, she has always been there, adopted years ago by Miss Havisham. Herbert does not like Estella, and he feels that she is hard, proud, and brought up to wreak revenge on all men for Miss Havisham. Pip explains his expectations briefly and mentions that there are to be no inquiries about who the benefactor is. Both young men suspect it is Miss Havisham. Herbert currently works in a counting-house, but is an aspiring "capitalist" who hopes to insure merchant ships and make his fortune someday. Pip doubts he will ever achieve this.

The following Monday, the two proceed to Hammersmith where Pip meets Matthew Pocket and the rest of the family. The many Pocket children are "tumbling up," growing up without much supervision or interest from Mrs. Pocket or her nurses. Mrs. Pocket greets Pip, is oblivious to everything around her, and resumes reading her book. Pip then meets the perplexed and confused Mr. Pocket, a man not in charge of anything going on in his household, least of all, his wife.

Commentary

Pip is suffering the second thoughts common to most people when getting used to a new place and as such, feels that London is overrated. There may be an undercurrent of guilt in this, a feeling of "I left Joe and the forge for this?" Guilt is strong in him when he notes how quickly he is able to put mental distance between himself and home. He has just arrived and it already seems like he left home months ago. Wemmick's surprise when Pip reaches to shake his hand is another indication life in London is different. Basic rituals of friendship and kindness are either overlooked or have been corrupted into a trying to get something from someone.

Character Insight

There are some redeeming qualities in the characters of Herbert Pocket and Jaggers. Herbert apologizes for his sparse quarters because he supports himself, saying that, even if his father could support him, he would not allow it. He is an honorable, hard-working man with dreams for his future. At this point in the story, Pip thinks Herbert will never achieve them because Pip does not recognize that having dreams is different than being a dreamer: Having dreams propels you to set goals and strive; being a dreamer leaves one in a fantasy world without earning anything. Jaggers is another honorable man. While not the warmest human being, he is genuinely caring because he is honest and straightforward. Jaggers misleads no one, and therefore helps people in his own way. His bringing Pip to Matthew Pocket helps the latter in his struggle to support his family, and Jaggers' honest expectation that Pip will get into debt is his indirect way of trying to warn Pip not to get carried away with the money.

Dickens depicts the polite manners of society in a humorous interchange between Pip and Herbert as they eat. The rules of society are ridiculed a bit as well, when Herbert observes that one can be a brewer and still be considered a gentleman, but if you are a baker, all hope is lost.

Theme

Satire of the treatment of children by their parents continues with Dickens' depiction of the Pocket household. Mrs. Pocket is self-absorbed, Mr. Pocket is oblivious, and the children are raising themselves. The element of secrecy is also evident in the secret marriage of Miss Havisham's father to his cook after Miss Havisham's mother died. Repetition of elements such as Jaggers throwing his finger and using his handkerchief, continue. New elements to watch for are the face casts in Jaggers' office and Wemmick's "post-office" mouth.

Glossary

the Cross Keys a real inn from the seventeenth century where coaches coming into London from the provinces would stop.

Little Britain street north of St. Paul's Cathedral with many law offices because of its proximity to the criminal courts.

hackney-coachman a hackney coach-driver. A hackney coach would be similar to a modern taxi in that you would hire it to take you somewhere, unlike the coaches coming into London from the provinces, which stopped at only certain stations or inns.

equipage a carriage, especially one with horses and liveried servants.

Smithfield a large, open square that was London's main cattle-market until 1852.

Bartholomew Close a narrow street near Bartholomew Church in the Smithfield area.

all otherth ith Cag-Maggerth cagmag is garbage, like rotting flesh, and this comment indicates that the speaker considers all other lawyers useless compared to Jaggers.

like the Bull in Cock Robin pulling at the bell rope a nursery-rhyme reference about a bullfinch offering to toll the bell at Cock Robin's funeral. Here, the man speaking to Jaggers is pulling at a lock of his hair, often done by a country person as a sign of respect to a member of the gentry.

outrunning the constable spending more money than you make.

mourning rings A custom at the time was to bequeath money to friends or relatives so that they could buy a ring to remember one by, usually inscribed with the initials of the deceased.

pottle a small basket. It can also be a pot or tankard capable of holding a pottle or half gallon of liquid. In this case, Herbert is carrying a pottle of strawberries, so the basket reference is probably the correct one.

bad courtier A courtier, originally an attendant at a royal court, refers here to someone who is adept at using flattery to get something or to win favor. Herbert's father is a bad courtier with Miss Havisham in that he does not flatter her but speaks the truth whether she likes it or not.

propitiate to appease someone.

the Harmonious Blacksmith a piece of music by G. F. Handel (1685–1759) that was supposedly based on a blacksmith's song that the composer overheard.

counting-house a building or office in which a firm keeps records, handles correspondence, and so on.

went upon 'Change the floor of the Royal Exchange—the London Stock Market. Lloyd's, a marine insurance business at the time, operated from this building.

fluey dusty.

Chapters 23–25 (Volume II, Chapters 4–6)

Summary

Mrs. Pocket believes herself to be of upper-class lineage and spends most of her time reading books about titles and nobility. The entire household is in the hands of the servants, who take advantage of the confusion by keeping the best food downstairs for themselves. The Pockets married young, which impaired Mr. Pocket's prospects at Cambridge where he had distinguished himself early in his life. He now works tutoring young men and doing some literary editing. The other two men studying with Mr. Pocket are Bentley Drummle and Startop. Dinner reveals the interactions in the household, which is general chaos, and Pip decides to split his time between the Pockets' Hammersmith home and Herbert's flat. Pip takes up rowing on the Thames with the other gentlemen in the house. He finds Startop to be a bright lively fellow, if a bit effeminate, and Drummle to be rather distasteful. Miss Havisham's toady relatives, Camilla Pocket and her husband, visit Matthew Pocket, and Pip notes that Camilla, Georgiana, and Sarah hate him. Mr. Pocket tells Pip that he is not destined for training in any profession, but is to be educated to hold his own in the company of prosperous young men.

A visit to Jaggers' office for money introduces Pip to Jaggers' way of dealing with people. Wemmick tells Pip that the two plaster face casts in the office are of former clients of Jaggers, made after they were hanged. Wemmick points out that his rings are gifts from former clients, also deceased, who gave them to Wemmick to remember them by. He considers them "portable property." Pip is invited to join Wemmick at his Walworth home some time and is advised to take note of Jaggers' housekeeper when Pip dines with the attorney. The housekeeper is described as "a wild beast tamed." Pip then accompanies Wemmick to court to see Jaggers "at it," intimidating both court magistrates and clients and "grinding the whole place in a mill."

Pip dines with Wemmick one evening at his Walworth home, where he meets Wemmick's father, referred to as the Aged Parent. He also meets a totally different Wemmick. At his home, the law clerk is gentle with his father, open, caring and warm—the opposite of his law-office demeanor. Wemmick's home is his castle, complete with a moat, a bridge, a turret, and a cannon to fire every night at nine o'clock. He has his own garden, a pig, and some rabbits and chickens, and continues to invent and improve on devices in his home and yard. Pip learns that Wemmick keeps the two parts of his life very separate. This is evident as the two men walk to London the next day, and Pip notes that as they went along Wemmick "got dryer and harder . . . and his mouth tightened into a post-office again."

Commentary

Dickens' pen of satire strikes again, both at parents' abuse of their children and the class structure of society. Mrs. Pocket is useless, ornamental, and absorbed in reading about her grandfather's "almost" title. She is oblivious to caring for her children, who fall on their heads, swallow pins, and endure other almost calamities. Mrs. Pocket is put out when a neighbor writes that the nurse was striking the baby and wishes the neighbors would mind their own business. Mr. Pocket alternates between wondering why his children are there and melting into giving them all money. His children just sort of "happened" and he is not in control enough to meet any of their emotional needs.

In contrast to Mrs. Pocket with her upper-class concerns and useless trivia is Wemmick, who is trying to support himself and his father on a meager income. Struggling to get by, he is, out of necessity, very interested in any "portable property" he can acquire. He is not greedy, but is realistic about his finances. Dickens shows that Wemmick is a creative and sensitive man who is stuck in the drudgery and soul-killing job of a law clerk. He has no choice because of his financial needs, so to keep from being emotionally crushed by the crime he has to deal with every day, Wemmick survives by keeping his home and office lives completely separate.

The characterizations emphasized here are Wemmick's "post-office mouth," a sure sign he is in his "London" personality, and the comparison of Bentley Drummle to Orlick—Drummle is a higher-class Orlick, both surly in temperament and always creeping in the shadows.

Glossary

mount to the Woolsack or roof himself in with a mitre this reference is to Mr. Matthew Pocket's possible career choices when he was young—he could have become either a lawyer or clergyman. As a lawyer he could aspire to become Lord Chancellor of England and sit upon the Woolsack in the House of Lords. As a clergyman he could hope to become a bishop and wear a mitre (the British spelling of miter, which is the peaked hat worn by bishops).

taken Time by the forelock seize the opportunity and act. The reference is Greek, from the philosopher Thales of Miletus (around 624–546 BC).

Grinder a private tutor who prepares students for their examinations.

dull blades a blade is an easy-going playboy. Dull would indicate that this student is not very smart.

serpentine something that twists or coils like a snake.

a Dutch doll a wooden doll with jointed legs, made in Germany.

Dying Gladiator Mr. Pocket, overwhelmed by the chaos in his house, drops down onto the sofa in this pose. It refers to "The Dying Gaul," a Roman copy of a Greek statue of a dying gladiator lying down propped up on one arm.

The cast was made in Newgate This term refers to the plaster face casts in Jaggers office, which were the death masks of two of his clients made right after they were hanged. These masks were often made after executions and sold to willing buyers.

gentlemanly Cove a gentlemanly chap or man.

Bounceable Here, Wemmick is talking to one of the plaster face casts and saying what a boaster and liar that client was.

Britannia metal cheap silverware made of tin and antimony and marked with an image of Britannia.

gold repeater Jaggers' watch. It repeats, meaning it chimes the last hour or quarter hour when a lever is pressed and thus it can be checked in the dark. Its use was not as important after sulfur matches became common.

bower a place enclosed by overhanging boughs of trees or by vines on a trellis.

tobacco-stoppers used to push tobacco into the bowl of a pipe.

a brazen bijou, a roasting-jack the first is a brass ring that holds the second, a device to turn a joint of meat on a spit over an open fire.

Chapters 26–28
(Volume II, Chapters 7–9)

Summary

Pip, Herbert, Drummle, and Startop meet Jaggers at his office because he has invited them to his house for dinner. Pip has previously seen Jaggers' cleaning ritual of meticulously washing his hands between court cases or clients. Today before heading home, the ritual is expanded. Jaggers not only washes his hands but also his face, gargles his throat, and uses a penknife to scrape under his nails. His home is stately but in need of paint and the windows need cleaning. Although it is quite large, he uses only three rooms. Everything is of fine quality, official, and solid, but nothing is fancy or ornamental.

Jaggers gets into the heads of his dinner guests, extracting their personalities from them during the course of dinner, wine, and conversation, like he might extract a confession from a suspect. He is especially interested in Drummle, and refers to him as the "Spider" or the "blotchy, sprawly, sulky fellow." Jaggers personally attends to his guests' drinks and condiments—the only other help is from his maid, who brings in the food for him to serve. Pip remembers Wemmick's mention of the strange maid and he observes that her face is disturbed. The young men drink too much and quarrel, revealing their personal differences. Promptly at nine-thirty, Jaggers announces he has work left to do and then proceeds to "wash off" his dinner guests.

Pip receives a note that Joe is coming to visit him — something he dreads. He is relieved Joe is coming to the Barnard Inn and not Hammersmith, where Joe would be subject to Drummle's judgments. Pip has been living high and spending too much, and he even has a servant now. Joe arrives and is ill at ease: He is out of character in his dress clothes, wipes his feet for what seems forever before coming in, fidgets with his hat (which keeps falling on the floor), and keeps calling Pip "Sir." On observing the closeness of the apartment, he wonders how they stay healthy and adds that he would not keep a pig there. His struggle with the fork, food, and table manners embarrasses Pip. Finally Joe delivers his message sent by Miss Havisham: Estella is back and would be glad to see him. Acknowledging that he and Pip are not meant to be together in London, Joe leaves shortly afterward. Pip, guilty, and realizing he did nothing to make the man comfortable, goes after him. But Joe is gone.

Pip catches a coach home, riding with two convicts who are being transferred to the Hulks. They do not recognize Pip, but he recognizes one of them as the man from the Jolly Bargemen with the shilling and the two one-pound notes. He overhears them talking about Pip's convict and that he was made a lifer. They arrive at the Blue Boar, where Pip has decided to stay for his visit. He had planned to see Joe, but keeps finding excuses to avoid the man. The waiter gives Pip a newspaper article about Pumblechook, who again proclaims himself Pip's first benefactor.

Commentary

Jaggers' life is his work, which is clear because his house is in need of repair. The fact that it is gloomy, furnished with only essentials, and that he only uses three rooms indicates he is a rational, functional type who does not indulge himself in ornamental things. At the dinner, Jaggers dissects the psyches of the young men, getting them to reveal their flaws. Drummle especially interests him and later Jaggers tells Pip he likes the man because Drummle is one of the "true sort." The lawyer's interest in Drummle is probably a professional one. Jaggers deals with the raw side of humanity every day working with the criminal, violent, unbridled types. Drummle, in spite of his family's station, is of the same mold and Jaggers finds him interesting, much as one may find it interesting to dissect an insect. The spider reference indicates as much, and alludes to a predatory nature. Jaggers shows a fatherly concern for Pip when he warns Pip to stay away from the man. A methodical, disciplined man, Jaggers promptly ends the dinner at nine-thirty to return to work, and Pip observes Jaggers washing his hands of them. The hand-washing, gargling, finger-nail cleaning ritual is likely Jaggers' way of separating himself from the criminal world of his office and from any emotional attachments in his life.

His maid is interesting, as she seems to have a wild nature that is strongly controlled by Jaggers. Her hands are powerful, the ugly scar on her wrist speaks to a violence in her past, yet she almost fearfully waits for Jaggers' every command.

Joe's visit is a nightmare for both Joe and Pip. Joe is not proud, but wants to be correct, so he is dressed in his uncomfortable Sunday clothes. He addresses Pip as "Sir," which irritates Pip. And he keeps fidgeting with his hat, which Pip refers to sarcastically in the book as the "bird's nest." Joe's lack of sophistication shows in his table manners and his assuming that his visiting the Blacking Warehouse constitutes seeing the sights of London. This warehouse, incidentally, is the horrible place Dickens had to work as a child. Joe is not a cardboard man, however, and does have opinions and angry emotions. When he is offered coffee, he accepts, but politely notes he prefers tea. He is angry with Pumblechook for going about town pretending that he was Pip's childhood playfellow, when in fact it was really Joe. It is interesting to note that Joe also adds, "though it signify little now, Sir." Joe knows things have changed, the past is past, and none of that means much anymore to Pip. Dickens infuses some humor at Pip's expense when Joe says that he would not keep a pig in their flat, and while, in saying so, Joe manages to irritate Pip, realistically, any reader would probably agree that the freedom of a pen on the open marshes would be healthier for anyone than a stifling London flat. Joe leaves with his dignity intact, delivering his message and departing quickly. He knows that he and Pip are not meant to spend time together in London and tells Pip that he will not be seen in those clothes again. They and London are not right for him, but Joe tells Pip to feel free to see him anytime on the forge. Joe correctly observes that seen there, he can be judged in a better light.

Theme

Guilt, shame, pride, snobbery—these are all running through Pip. Pip is demeaning to Herbert at Jaggers' dinner, his attitude demeans Joe during his visit, and although Pip has another moment of decency and insight when he runs after Joe, it is useless. Joe has already gone and it is too late to apologize to him. Pip has a way of waiting just long enough to not have to be honorable. And any good thoughts are again wiped away when he finds excuses not to visit Joe when he goes home to see Miss Havisham. The taint of crime continues to follow Pip when he shares a coach with two convicts. Try as he might to be upper class, Pip just cannot seem to escape his lower-class criminal connections.

Glossary

capacious dumb-waiter a piece of furniture with shelves to hold sauces, silverware, and other items for dinner.

faces out of the Witches' caldron a reference to Act IV, Scene 1 of Shakespeare's Macbeth. Macbeth visits the witches as they stir their caldron, and he demands an explanation of their prophecies about him. They ask if he wants the story from them or from their masters, and he asks to see their masters. The witches promptly work their magic and a number of apparitions arise from the boiling caldron.

in the books of a neighboring upholsterer . . . a boy in boots Pip is in debt to a local interior decorator and furniture dealer. He has also hired a servant.

Provincial Amateur of Roscian renown . . . our National Bard Quintus Roscius Gallus (died 62 BC) was the greatest Roman comic actor of his time, so this reference indicates an actor of the same level of renown. Our National Bard refers to Shakespeare. Essentially, the playbill from the small theater is claiming Wopsle to be a great actor who is performing in a Shakespearean play.

a peck of orange-peel Joe's comment here indicates the audience threw a lot of orange peels, essentially expressing their dislike of the performance.

pettishly peevishly, petulantly, crossly.

bread-poultice, baize, rope-yarn, and hearthstone these references apply to the convicts that rode with Pip to the Hulks. Bread-poultice was bread soaked in hot water, put in cloth, and applied to bruises and swellings. Baize was a cheap, thick wool cloth probably used for prison clothes. Rope-yarn refers to the fact that prisoners were often put to work unraveling old rope. Hearthstone refers to stone broken up to use to whiten doorsteps and hearthstones.

the Mentor of our young Telemachus . . . Quintin Matsys . . . VERB. SAP." The waiter at the Blue Boar, who assumes Pip owes everything to Pumblechook, hands Pip this newspaper article that Pumblechook has run. Telemachus was the young son of Odysseus who was guided during his father's absence by Athene, disguised as an old friend of his father's. Quintin Matsys was a Flemish painter who supposedly began his career as a blacksmith. VERB. SAP. is a Latin abbreviation for verbum satis sapienti, meaning "a hint is enough to the wise." Pumblechook is claiming to be the great mentor and first benefactor of someone and is saying that a good hint is all they need to figure out who the young man is. He provides the hint with the reference to the Flemish painter who was first a blacksmith.

Chapters 29–31 (Volume II, Chapters 10–12)

Summary

Pip is convinced that Miss Havisham intends to adopt him and have him marry Estella. He sees himself as the knight in shining armor bringing sunshine into that house and their lives. Orlick is now working as Miss Havisham's guard and Pip is nervous when Orlick points out the loaded gun with the brass-bound stock over the chimney. Estella is even more beautiful than before and Pip is again under the spell of the place and the old influences. She tells Pip that his old companions will not do with his new image, which convinces him to avoid Joe. She also warns him that she loves no one, not even him, and to believe her in this. But as Pip wheels Miss Havisham around the rooms, he observes that the enchantment is even stronger now. Miss Havisham revels in her revenge and urges him to love Estella no matter how she treats him. Jaggers arrives for dinner along with Sarah Pocket, who is still green with envy about Pip. Before Pip leaves, Miss Havisham tells him that Estella will be coming to London and he will be notified so that he can escort her.

The next morning, Pip breakfasts with Jaggers and mentions his fears about Orlick. Jaggers decides to fire the man, much to Pip's discomfort. On his way to catch the London coach, Pip runs into Trabb's boy. The tailor's assistant makes a spectacle of mocking Pip and drawing attention to him. Pip manages to escape but when he is back in London, he writes an angry letter to Trabb telling him he will not do business with a man who employs such a poor assistant. Also, because his conscience is bothering him, Pip sends Joe a penitential codfish and barrel of oysters. Herbert tries in vain to talk Pip out of pursuing Estella, but as usual, Pip cannot let go even though he knows Estella is wrong for him. Herbert tells Pip about his fiancée, Clara, and how he cannot marry her yet because he has no money. Pip has his own money worries because he does not know who his benefactor is and how much money he is to get, and because he has no formal job training, what he will do if he loses it. To soothe their depressed hearts, they go out to see Wopsle perform in a play.

Commentary

The chapter with Wopsle's play is mostly a side show that Dickens puts in for humor. The thread about Wopsle is there so that later in the book he can warn Pip that Compeyson is trailing him. Tags such as references to thick boots, being coarse and common, and Sarah Pocket as Pip's green and yellow friend continue, and the secrecy theme is seen in Herbert's keeping his engagement to Clara a secret from his mother. There are again references to the fantasy theme. Pip talks about being under the spell and enchantment of the old influences and sees himself as the knight of romance who will "admit sunshine into the dark rooms, set the clocks a going and the cold hearths a blazing." He also worries about losing his money, because he cannot support himself and he believes that money is the key to Estella.

Pip is obsessed with Estella. He knows it and Herbert knows it, but nothing can stop Pip. This is addiction, not love. Miss Havisham's definition of love is the best clue. What she describes is a sick dependency, not genuine caring, and the old woman revels in Pip's response to Estella. There is no question that she is beautiful, and even Jaggers steals a glance at Estella during the card game. Pip has no identity of his own because he has no goal in life other than to please Miss Havisham and love Estella. He snubs Joe to please them.

Pip is also a coward who deals with people "long distance." He avoids Joe when he is home, so he soothes his conscience by sending the man a barrel of oysters. He manages to get Orlick fired, but it is Jaggers who does the dirty work of firing him. His complaints about Trabb's boy are sent in a letter. Pip doesn't face the people he hurts or the consequences of his actions, and if he does, he acts like a victim. When Pip complains about his servant, it sounds like the servant is in control, not Pip. His complaints seem similar to those of the adults around him when he was a boy. Pip is Pumblechook. By comparison, Estella seems downright caring when she warns Pip not to love her. She is, at least, honest and forthright.

Glossary

Tag and Rag and Bobtail riff-raff or rabble.

whist a card game that was the forerunner to bridge.

being insured in some extraordinary Fire Office at that time, fire insurance companies put plaques on the buildings they insured. They also had their own fire engine companies. When the fire companies were racing to a fire, the emblem on the building let them know if it was one of their buildings to save.

Chapters 32–34 (Volume II, Chapters 13–15)

Summary

Pip arrives five hours early at the coach-office to meet Estella. Wemmick happens by and invites Pip to join him on a trip to Newgate, where Pip notes that the prisoners' conditions are not good. He watches Wemmick attend to the many who seek him out, as a gardener tends to his plants. Pip begins to understand that even though Wemmick maintains an air of Jaggers' reserve about him, he is the one who brings a touch of humanity to each client connection. Even when he tells clients who cannot pay that they need to find another attorney, he is caring because he is honest and encourages no false hopes. One of their clients, the Colonel, is to be executed because the evidence against him was too great even for Jaggers to save him. Yet the Colonel tells Wemmick he wishes he had enough money so that Wemmick could buy a ring to remember him by. Wemmick responds by asking for a couple of the man's pigeons, because pigeons are portable property as well. Pip is impressed by the way the guards treat Wemmick, and the esteem they have for Jaggers. However, upon returning to the coach-office, Pip regrets the side trip because he now feels tainted by crime in the presence of his angel, Estella.

Estella orders Pip about, matter-of-factly listing exactly what they are to do as if it has already been laid out for her and him. In fact, she tells Pip that they are not free to follow their own devices. As he escorts her to the place she will stay, they talk about Miss Havisham's toady relatives and he notes her strong reaction to them. They apparently made her childhood miserable and she is grateful to Pip because he causes them a great deal of misery through their jealousy of him. However, she again reminds him not to get attached to her and that they are mere puppets.

Pip and Herbert have joined a club of useless men called "The Finches of the Grove," who get together to eat expensive dinners and to quarrel. The two young men are seriously in debt and when they periodically panic about this, they arrange an elaborate dinner to sit down and go over the bills. Instead of paying them, they list and round off the amounts, then give themselves a "margin" to add on to the total debt, a margin they end up spending as well. Pip realizes he is dragging Herbert down with him and that at this rate, Herbert's dreams will never be reached. He also knows that if they were not such good friends they would hate each other. Pip takes his frustrations out on the Avenger, a servant boy Pip employs. The Avenger, according to Pip, does little but eat Pip's food. However on this morning, the boy's only crime is to offer Pip a roll for breakfast, yet Pip responds by grabbing him by the collar, lifting him off his feet, and shaking him. The chapter ends with a note from Trabb and Co. that Mrs. Joe has died and Pip's presence is requested for the next Monday's interment.

Commentary

When Wemmick runs into Pip outside the coach-office, Pip inquires about Wemmick's home and the Aged Parent. Wemmick chats a bit about them, but then reminds Pip that "this is not London talk." He is firm in keeping his two lives separate, although he pushes his limits more when talking to Pip than he does with anyone else.

Literary Device

Dickens uses the very effective plant metaphors when showing Wemmick talking to the clients in prison. Wemmick is the gardener, the prison is the greenhouse, the prisoners are the various plants, and the Colonel is the dead plant. The issues of mourning rings and portable property come up again when the Colonel, unable to buy a ring for Wemmick, agrees to give the clerk two pigeons. When one's finances are limited, even pigeons are portable property. Jaggers' renown in the prison both impresses and unnerves Pip. At times, he wishes he had a guardian of lesser abilities.

Pip is irrational, as usual, where Estella is concerned. Hearing she is coming to London, he regrets there is no time to have several new suits made, and he arrives five hours early to meet her. The taint of prison and crime continues to plague him and he feels contaminated in her presence after his visit to Newgate. He makes himself feel better when he demeans the waiter who brings Estella's tea. Regarding Estella, he continues to know she is wrong for him, observing that everything they do together gives him pain. He spends every minute dreaming of being with her and when he is, is it sheer agony. Estella continues to be honest in her warnings to him. Her mention of gratitude to him for making Miss Havisham's relatives miserable does give insight to her strange loyalty to him and a glimpse of an unhappy childhood.

Theme

Satire of abusive parents continues. Mrs. Pocket appears unconcerned for her baby's health after the baby seems to have ingested some pins. Her only response is to send the baby to bed. Pip himself is crossing a line of abusive behavior. Stressed about his finances, Pip complains about his servant, the Avenger, constantly. Instead of taking action and just firing the boy to save money, Pip acts as though he is the victim. Finally, one day when his frustrations peak over his debts, Pip grabs the boy and shakes him, acting abusive just like his sister did.

The social theme of prison reform is alluded to by the description of prison conditions at Newgate.

Glossary

set fire to their prisons . . . improving the flavour of their soup prison conditions were terrible in the early 1800s and reform was years off. By 1861, the outrage and reform had gone in the other direction, with prisoners rioting because they did not like their food. This pun refers to the fact that, at the time of this story, everyone's food was bad, whether prisoner, soldier, or pauper, so prisoners had not gotten to the point of rioting to "improve the flavour of their soup." Flavour is the British spelling for the word "flavor."

potman; prisoners buying beer prisoners were allowed all the beer they wanted in prison so long as they could pay the potman, someone from a local tavern who came to the prison to sell beer.

cistern a large receptacle for storing water; especially, a tank, usually underground in which rainwater is collected for use.

a Coiner a counterfeiter.

Moses in the bullrushes . . . butter in a quantity of parsley the appearance of a bit of butter nestled in a quantity of parsley reminds Pip of the baby Moses hidden in the bullrushes to escape Pharaoh's soldiers. This is from the Bible, Exodus 2:3.

ostler a person who takes care of horses at an inn, stable, and so on.

chary wary, careful.

Here is the green farthingale . . . and the blue solitaire a farthingale is a hooped petticoat worn by ladies in the early eighteenth century. The solitaire was a wide tie or cravat worn by men in the same period. These are no longer in fashion in Pip's time. This reference indicates the house is old and has seen its share of stately parties for many generations.

Chapters 35–37
(Volume II, Chapters 16–18)

Summary

Pip attends his sister's funeral, run by Mr. Trabb. It is a ridiculous affair, with grown men wrapped in cloaks with large bows tied under their chins. Joe is careful at dinner to properly use his knife and fork but is more relaxed when he goes outside with Pip to smoke his pipe. He is delighted when Pip asks to stay in his old room and Pip feels pleased with himself. Pip has some harsh words with Biddy as to why she did not write him about things. She calls him Mr. Pip now, and she stands her ground. She also lets Pip know that Orlick is working in a quarry and hangs around watching them. They have more angry words after she questions his resolve to visit Joe more often. When he leaves the next day, he tells her he is hurt, but as he leaves town he suspects she is right.

Back in London, Pip comes of age. Jaggers tells Pip he is aware of Pip's debts. He also gives him a five-hundred-pound note for his birthday from his benefactor and tells him his financial affairs are now in his own hands. He will get 125 pounds per quarter to spend as he sees fit, until such time as the benefactor makes himself known. At that point, Jaggers' connection in all this is over. Jaggers comes to dinner at Pip's apartment to celebrate his birthday, but the attorney's presence leaves both Pip and Herbert in a melancholy and guilty frame of mind.

Pip has an idea about using some of his money to set Herbert up in business. He seeks the advice of the Walworth Wemmick, because the London version of Wemmick suggested that Pip instead toss the money into the river from a bridge. On Sunday, Pip visits Wemmick at home where he learns the man actually trained to be a wine-cooper, not a legal clerk. He also meets Wemmick's lady friend, Miss Skiffins, who appears to also be in the "post-office branch of the service and possessed of portable property." The Walworth Wemmick is in favor of Pip's idea to help Herbert and agrees to contact Miss Skiffins' brother, who is an accountant. Wemmick notes that this helps to brush away some of the Newgate cobwebs. Within a short time they arrange things with a merchant named Clarriker who soon brings Herbert into his firm. All of this is done without Herbert's knowledge. Pip, the narrator, ends the chapter with a foreshadowing comment about the turning point of the story, but defers for one chapter to talk about Estella.

Commentary

Literary Device

The element of secrecy shows up here with Pip's secretly setting Herbert up in business with Clarriker. Character tags continue with: Pumblechook's "May I?" and his being the "founder of Pip's fortunes," Joe's "she were a fine figure of a woman" and "Pip, old chap," Jaggers' handwashing, and Wemmick's post-office mouth. Guilt is evident when both Pip and Herbert feel melancholy and guilty just by being around Jaggers for dinner. Herbert sums it up when he notes that he must be guilty of something but just cannot remember it. The feeling of impending evil is suggested by the presence of Orlick lurking in the shadows near the forge and following Pip and Biddy. It seems to foreshadow that the man has something ominous in store for someone. Another interesting element is Dickens use of inanimate objects to show the emotions of one of the characters. Pip is frequently attributing his own emotions to the face casts in Jaggers' office: " . . . the twitched faces looked, . . . as if they had come to a crisis . . . and were going to sneeze."

Theme

Money as a source of good and evil is also at issue. Money has done little good for Pip or Herbert—both are deeply in debt and the problem threatens to wipe out Herbert's dreams. Yet Pip still has good in him. Realizing he is the main corrupting influence on Herbert, he fixes things by setting Herbert up in business. Also, Jaggers attempts to guide Pip when he cross-examines Pip about his debts. Jaggers tells the young man that he has been irresponsible, does not let Pip lie to him, and tries to make him straighten up because Pip is now in charge of his own affairs. Jaggers is trying to help Pip mature.

The dynamics of steadfast friendship and betrayal are still operating with Pip, Joe, and Biddy. Pip does return for his sister's funeral and pleases Joe by asking to stay there. The old rapport is stressed in that Joe is very particular about his silverware use when Pip is around and he continues to call him "Sir." No doubt that Pip genuinely means to keep his word when he tells Biddy that he will visit Joe frequently now, and he is angry when she doubts him. However, as Pip leaves town, he suspects she is right. She knows him.

Split Wemmicks are again evident when Pip seeks advice about helping Herbert in business. Just as there is London and Walworth, Jaggers and the Aged, there is professional money advice and personal money advice. Wemmick does stretch his rule of separating the two places for Pip again though, when he helps with some of the business details for Herbert's position even while in London.

Glossary

came of age the age of majority. Pip is now considered an adult.

injudicious showing poor judgment; not discreet or wise.

wine-cooper someone involved in the retail wine trade, especially making, repairing, or filling wine barrels. This was Wemmick's first trade, a far cry from his current legal work.

Chapters 38 and 39
(Volume II, Chapters 19–20)

Summary

Estella's attitude toward Pip remains unchanged and her warnings not to care for her continue. She tells him that she deceives and entraps all men but him. Pip accompanies her on a number of visits to Satis House, which continue to be painful because of Miss Havisham's vengefulness and Estella's indifference. Pip concludes that Miss Havisham will not make Estella his until she has had enough revenge. On one of these visits, Pip witnesses an argument between the two women. Estella is tired of Miss Havisham's clinging and pulls back. Hurt, Miss Havisham accuses her of being ungrateful and unloving. Estella points out that she is grateful and obedient but that giving love is the one thing she cannot do as she was not taught it. Miss Havisham is miserable and it becomes apparent that her plans have backfired. While Pip never again sees the two women argue, he notices an element of fear in Miss Havisham now. He is also upset because, as he discovers on his return to London, Drummle has been courting Estella.

At twenty-three, Pip has completed his time with Mr. Pocket, and now lives with Herbert in a flat at the Temple, a building near the Thames mostly occupied by lawyers and law students. He is unable to stick with anything except reading, and is restless and uncertain about his future and his wealth. Herbert is doing well with Clarriker and is away on business. The weather has been wretched, cold, and stormy and on one particularly miserable night, a stranger arrives at Pip's home. The stranger knows Pip's name and is happy to see him. Pip is at first afraid of the stranger, then repulsed when he recognizes the man is his convict from years ago. The convict is pleased to see how well Pip has grown and thrilled to see he is such a gentleman. Pip encourages him to leave, but seeing tears in the man's eyes, softens, and offers him a drink. In the course of their conversation, the convict reveals that he is the source of Pip's expectations, his way of rewarding Pip for helping him on the marshes. He wanted to make Pip a gentleman who could live an easy, upper-class life. Pip is revolted and depressed. He realizes now that Miss Havisham is not his benefactor, Estella can never be his, and worst of all, he has deserted Joe for the money of a convict. He is also fearful because the convict came back to England to see Pip and will be hanged if he's caught.

Commentary

Theme

"Money as power" is a dominant theme in these chapters. Pip escorts Estella to Satis House and always, she pays. By not allowing Pip to pay, Estella controls the situation and is beholden to no one. Whoever holds the money, therefore, holds the control. The convict holds the power over Pip because he is the benefactor. His money has provided Pip's easy life and, prepared for no other profession, Pip has become totally dependent on that money. Pip's blind pursuit of money to win Estella has also cost him Joe. He has traded Joe for the convict—the guilt and shame nearly crush Pip.

The reader senses a fair bit of hinting and foreshadowing in these chapters, as when Dickens ends Chapter 19 with a tale of ceilings falling in on Pip. Something bad is about to happen. Also, before Magwitch actually reveals that he is Pip's benefactor, he drops a number hints to give Pip the chance to guess this fact.

The fantasy descriptions of Miss Havisham continue. She has also become the victim of her own madness. Estella tells her and Pip that she is incapable of loving anyone because that has been her training. Miss Havisham never intended for that weapon of revenge to wound her, as well as the young men that Estella rejects. Yet, Estella is being as kind as she is capable of through her openness and honesty. She is dutiful, grateful, generous, and obedient to Miss Havisham but she cannot love her. Miss Havisham is now afraid of her own creation. With Pip, Estella shows her own sense of caring and fairness, a kind of loyalty. She does not use him the way she uses all other men and she continually reinforces her warnings to him. Pip's constant unhappiness in her presence remains unchanged yet he cannot pull away. He is also sickened watching Miss Havisham's desperate clinging to Estella. In a moment of insight, he sees his obsession as a dark, sick thing and feels dependent, degraded, controlled, but is unable to pull out of it. He resents Drummle's seeing Estella and the spider metaphor returns in descriptions of Drummle's movements around Estella.

Glossary

fête days festival days or days with gala parties held outdoors.

he knew where I was to be found Pip is so upset when Drummle toasts Estella at a meeting of the Finches and tells everyone he is acquainted with her, that Pip challenges him to a duel. The Finches arrange a bloodless way to resolve the fight with Drummle producing a certificate from the lady proving his acquaintance and Pip apologizing when he does.

In the Eastern story . . . the ceiling fell from a book Dickens read as a boy, *Tales of the Genii*, with stories similar to the *Arabian Nights*. The sixth tale in this book has the wise vizier for the sultan foiling the sultan's enemies with an elaborate trap like the one mentioned here. A stone crushes the enemies as they sleep. The point is that the enemies thought they were at the peak of their power having trapped the sultan, and suddenly their luck ran out. The same is about to happen to Pip.

"It's death to come back." These words spoken by the convict to Pip set the main danger and conflict for the rest of the novel. However, the direness of the convict's situation was most likely nowhere near as bad as Dickens makes it out to be in the book. The last time someone hanged for returning to England after being banished was in 1810. From 1827–1830, out of eight returned convicted transports, none was executed. By 1834, the death penalty for illegal reentry had been taken off the statute books.

Chapters 40–42
(Volume III, Chapters 1–3)

Summary

Pip feels a mixture of revulsion for the convict and fear for the convict's safety. Apparently, someone followed the convict the night he arrived at Pip's apartment and later Pip stumbles over someone hiding in the dark at the bottom of his apartment stairs. While the convict has come to England to see Pip and enjoy flaunting the gentleman he has made, Pip tells him he is in danger and that they need to lay low. The convict tells Pip his name is Abel Magwitch and that he is using the name "Provis" for this trip. He suggests that Pip tell everyone he is Pip's uncle.

Pip visits Jaggers to seek advice. Jaggers is careful to prevent Pip from saying that "Magwitch" is in England so they cannot be accused of breaking the law. He also confirms that Miss Havisham is not Pip's benefactor. All business, the lawyer tells Pip he will forward all accounts and balances due, so that Pip may communicate this information to this "Provis" person, or by mail to Magwitch in *New South Wales*.

Pip secures an apartment nearby for Magwitch and orders some clothes for a disguise. However no matter what Magwitch puts on, he has "convict" written all over him. Pip is thrilled when Herbert returns. The convict swears Herbert to secrecy and it is obvious from Herbert's face that he shares Pip's feelings. Later, when the convict has gone to his lodging, Pip and Herbert discuss what to do. They agree Pip can no longer accept the man's money, and that Pip must get him out of England as soon as possible. In the course of making plans, they learn from Magwitch that he was abandoned early in childhood and barely survived. He tells them about his involvement in crime but assures them he has paid his debt to society and will not be "low." He mentions working with two men, Arthur and Compeyson, the latter having swindled some money years before from some rich lady. Compeyson and Magwitch eventually ended up on the same prison ship but Compeyson got off easy being a gentleman. Magwitch, on the other hand, was sentenced to life, and then banished. Herbert tells Pip that Miss Havisham's brother's name was Arthur and Compeyson was the man who left her at the altar.

Commentary

Literary
Device

Wemmick and Jaggers display their careful habit of staying just within the law by referring to Provis as an agent of Magwitch, who they are "sure" is in Australia. They are careful in all their statements so that no one can trace them to the knowledge that Magwitch is in England illegally. Ominous events are foreshadowed when Pip suspects that Magwitch has been followed to his apartment and that someone is now watching them.

Magwitch's motives are a mixture of good and bad; part reward, part revenge. He is obviously grateful for Pip's help years ago and is generously rewarding him with an easy life. Even his manner of holding Pip's hands is much more honest and heartfelt than Pumblechook's "May I?" However Magwitch can be "low" as well. He wants to show society that a low dog like him can make a fine gentleman. By showing Pip off to the world he gets revenge for how the world treated him.

Pip's and Herbert's reactions to Magwitch's money are interesting and somewhat snobbish. Pip is essentially dependent, living off of someone else's money. Whose money it is should not make any difference—he is dependent no matter what. But even though the money is honestly earned, Pip cannot bring himself to accept the convict's gift. In one respect it is a good decision because finally Pip is deciding to fend for himself and to care for another out of higher motives than money. But at the same time, refusing the gift solely because of who gives it is sheer snobbery.

Dickens continues to show his skills in the descriptive scenes of Magwitch's eating habits, and the use of the face casts in Jaggers' office to reflect Pip's thoughts and feelings.

Glossary

Negro-head tobacco strong black tobacco sweetened with molasses and pressed into square cakes that was popular with sailors and workingmen.

hair powder; shorts Magwitch's suggestions for a disguise are out-dated, reflecting his many years away from England. Wigs were no longer used, hair powder was used only by the old-fashioned, and shorts or knee-breeches were worn only by some clergy members on ceremonial occasions.

physiognomy the practice of trying to judge character and mental qualities by observation of bodily, especially facial, features.

pannikins small pans or metal cups.

the crimes in the Calendar this is a reference to the Newgate Calendar (1771), a series of true-crime stories. Pip is imaging that Magwitch's crimes were among these.

kind of Patience solitaire.

fashionable crib . . . a shake-down Magwitch wants Pip to find him cheap lodging of the kind thieves are used to, often in disreputable public-houses where the beds are made up of straw on the floor.

a Traveller's Rest a place that tramps, convicts, or people in hiding (such as a deserting soldier) would have used for a shelter.

the horrors the last stage of alcoholism: delirium tremens.

Bridewells and Lock-Ups prisons.

Chapters 43–45
(Volume III, Chapters 4–6)

Summary

Pip visits Estella and Miss Havisham one last time before leaving to get Magwitch out of the country. He meets Drummle at the Blue Boar and is angered by Drummle's boasting that he is having dinner with Estella. Pip is received with surprise at Satis House and he gets right to the point. Telling them he knows his benefactor and that it will do him no good in enriching his station, reputation, or wealth, he admonishes Miss Havisham for hurting him by leading him to believe she was the source of his expectations. While he was treated fairly with the apprenticeship he knows he served her purpose in antagonizing her toady relatives. She flashes an angry response telling him he made his own snare, but continues to listen. Pip tells her how honorable Herbert and Matthew Pocket have been in contrast to the other relatives. Explaining that he can no longer accept his inheritance he would appreciate Miss Havisham providing the rest of the payment for Herbert's business and to keep this a secret.

Pip then tells Estella that he knows he will never have her and does not blame Miss Havisham, as he does not believe she realized what she was doing. When Estella tells him she is going to marry Drummle, Pip passionately pleads with her to marry anyone else, at least someone worthy of her. Estella is unmoved, but Miss Havisham's distraught face is suddenly filled with shock, pity, and remorse. Pip leaves and decides to walk back to London. Reaching the Temple about midnight, he is given a note from Wemmick telling him not to go home.

He spends a sleepless night at Hummums in Covent Garden, where a bed is always available to travelers. Early in the morning he heads for Wemmick's house. The clerk tells him that an unnamed person is in danger and being watched. He tells Pip that he and Herbert moved that certain person to the house where Herbert's fiancée boards. He advises Pip to use the big city to lay low until things quiet down, and then get the person out of town. Telling Pip to make tonight Pip's only visit there, he advises Pip to get hold of the portable property tonight. Pip succeeds in pushing the Walworth Wemmick a bit further to confirm that Compeyson is still alive and living in London.

Commentary

Dickens has some fun with his characters when he has Drummle and Pip acting like two children vying for power in front of the Blue Boar's fireplace. He also foreshadows the type of death Drummle will have by showing his brutal treatment of his horse in this chapter.

The element of portraying emotions through an object shows up in these chapters through Dickens' description of the bed Pip gets at Hummums as a despotic monster that squeezes all the other furniture in the room.

Orlick surfaces again as the man who lights Drummle's cigar outside the inn. While not mentioned specifically, the slouching shoulders and ragged hair point to Orlick and give the feeling that Pip is surrounded by evil that is closing in on him. This feeling is compounded by the note Wemmick leaves at the Temple warning Pip not to go home, and Wemmick's later telling Pip he and Magwitch are being watched.

Wemmick, utilizing his knowledge of criminal elements and his law clerk talents for detail, manages to hide Magwitch and instructs Pip and Herbert how to keep the man hidden and plot his escape. Wemmick thinks of everything right down to leaving notes for Pip at all gates of the Temple and then returning to retrieve the extras. He understands about leaving no trails of incriminating evidence. Portable property is emphasized again when Wemmick tells Pip to get his hands on it. He is frank in saying they do not know what will happen to Magwitch. It is interesting that for all his effort to keep his two lives separate, Wemmick is mixing both places together more than he ever has, to save Magwitch. He conveys London information at Walworth, and acts, motivated by his Walworth kindness, when in London.

Miss Havisham's transformation has started. She shows fierce anger when Pip points out how she has hurt him, her first open expression of a charged emotion. But as she listens to his impassioned pleas to Estella, sees his willingness to even give up Estella as long as she is happy, Miss Havisham is filled with pity and remorse. Pip's directness to both Miss Havisham and Estella in stating his feelings and insights are a change as well. Instead of being a passive victim, he is calling things as he sees them and demanding certain actions. The secrecy theme continues when Pip asks Miss Havisham to take over helping Herbert and to keep it between the two of them.

Estella shows some interesting insight regarding her choice of Drummle as a husband. She observes to Pip that she cannot give herself to a man who would recognize she has nothing to offer him in the way of love, and assures Pip she will not be a blessing to Drummle. It is a negative thing either way, though: Either she is in power and Drummle will suffer or Drummle will rule and she will feel the pain. In either event, someone will get hurt.

Glossary

walk all the way to London from Pips' home area, this was a distance of about twenty-six miles.

superscription something, such as an address or name, written at the top or on an outer surface of an envelope or similar item.

Hummums in Covent Garden a place at the southeast corner of Covent Garden that was the site of one of England's earliest Turkish baths. During the eighteenth century, it was a combination steam bath, eatery, health center, and brothel; later it was a hotel.

rush-light a cheap candle made from the pith of the stem of a rush that has been dipped in grease and fat instead of wax. At Hummums, these were put in a perforated tin holder that left a dotted pattern of light on the walls.

close the eyes of the foolish Argus at Hummums, Pip cannot sleep any better than the Greek mythological giant, Argus. The giant had one hundred eyes, fifty of which were open even while he slept.

Chapters 46–48
(Volume III, Chapters 7–9)

Summary

After spending the day resting at Wemmick's house, Pip heads out to see Magwitch. He meets Clara, Herbert's fiancée, and her father, Mr. Barley, an alcoholic retired ship's purser who is close to death. Magwitch, under the name of Campbell, occupies two bright and airy rooms at the top of the house. Pip notices that he seems much "softer" now, a change Pip cannot figure out.

Magwitch, Pip, and Herbert discuss what to do. It is agreed that Magwitch remain there in hiding. When the time is right, Pip and Magwitch will go abroad. Herbert suggests that he and Pip get a boat and start rowing on the river to establish that as part of their routine. Then they can get Magwitch on board a ship without involving anyone else. Magwitch will signal from the window with the blinds when he sees them, to let them know he is well. As the weeks wear on and there is no word from Wemmick about when to leave, Pip's affairs start to get dire. He sells some of his jewelry to pay his bills. To kill some time, Pip goes to the theater one evening to see Mr. Wopsle's latest theatrical failure. He notices Wopsle staring intently at him during one scene and later learns that Wopsle was staring at the man right behind him. He is the same man Pip and Wopsle saw fighting with Pip's convict on the marshes years ago. Realizing the man is Compeyson, Pip knows he is being followed and sends a note to Wemmick at Walworth.

About a week later, Jaggers invites Pip to dine with Wemmick and him. Jaggers has a note for Pip from Miss Havisham, and through very dry hints from Wemmick, Pip understands to see her tomorrow. Jaggers notes that the Spider has won the pool, meaning Drummle has married Estella, and observes that the winner of the power play between the two has yet to be decided. He observes that a man like Drummle either beats or cringes, and toasts to the success of Mrs. Bentley Drummle. Molly comes in at that moment and some action of her fingers suddenly trips a memory in Pip of Estella's fingers when she was knitting. He realizes that Molly is Estella's mother.

On the way home, Wemmick tells Pip how Molly was on trial years ago for murdering an older, stronger woman who was allegedly having an affair with Molly's husband. Jaggers was her lawyer, and this case is the one that actually made him successful. He artfully dressed her to look weaker than she was, made no comment about her strong hands, and proved the scratches on her hands were from bramble bushes not a struggle. Also it was said Molly murdered her child to get even with her husband, but Jaggers was able to sway the jury away from that opinion. Molly has worked for Jaggers ever since.

Commentary

Dickens often cast the children in his stories as orphans, perhaps due to the abandonment he felt as a child. That trend continues in this book with Pip who is an orphan, and Estella, Clara, and Herbert who have living parents that are either unknown or useless to them. The foreshadowing of evil continues when Pip detects that Compeyson is following him.

Literary Device

Other elements that repeat in these chapters are the "emotional" face casts in Jaggers' office; Jaggers' handwashing, letter-writing, candle-snuffing, and safe-locking routines; the spider metaphor with Drummle (nicknamed "the spider") winning Estella; and the twin Wemmick's and his post-office mouth. New elements are the pieces of Molly's story falling into place and Pip's realization that she is Estella's mother. Jaggers' comment about the power struggle between Drummle and Estella, and his prophetic mention of Drummle beating or cringing, foreshadows the outcome of that struggle.

Glossary

Pool below Bridge the area downriver from, or east of, London Bridge.

Mill Pond Bank, Chink's Basin; the Old Green Copper Rope-Walk these locations are likely fictitious. The last one means "the place where ropes used to be made out of oxidized copper wire." However, at this time, copper wire was not used in ropes yet. Another meaning is the long narrow shed or roofed over alley where ropemakers twisted hemp strands into rope.

chandler's shop originally, a shop specializing in candles; here, it refers to a general store, which would also stock candles. A chandler was, originally, a maker or seller of candles.

Double Gloucester a thick, creamy cheese that is twice as large and old as regular Gloucester. Herbert's concern here is that the old man will hurt himself trying to cut through it.

Geographical chop-house . . . porter-pot a less-than-clean restaurant serving beefsteaks and mutton-chops and catering to clientele who are not concerned with neat eating habits. The porter-pot was a pot for holding cheap, bitter, dark-brown beer named for the people who drank it—porters and workingmen.

pudding in the cloth a dinner made by putting a flour mixture in a pudding bag, sometimes adding meat or vegetables, and boiling it.

young person in bed-furniture the person's clothes appear to be made from the curtains off of a four-poster bed.

swab a lowly seaman.

black gaiters cloth or leather coverings for the insteps and ankles, and, sometimes, the calves of the legs; also, spats or leggings.

plenipotentiary a person, especially a diplomatic agent, given full authority to act as representative of a government.

dance a hornpipe lively dance played on a hornpipe, which is an obsolete wind instrument with a bell and mouthpiece made of horn.

sententious tending to use a lot of maxims or proverbs and often inclined to moralize more than is appreciated.

antipodes that is, through a trapdoor.

necromantic work book of black magic or sorcery.

game at Bo-Peep Pip is referring to the plaster casts in Jaggers' office that, in the shadowy reflections of the fire, look as if they are playing peekaboo with him. This is another example of human actions or emotions ascribed to inanimate objects.

over the broomstick a folk marriage ceremony, essentially one with no legal status. Because Estella's parents were married this way, she is illegitimate.

Chapters 49–51
(Volume III, Chapters 10–12)

Summary

In response to Miss Havisham's note, Pip visits her the next day, and though she has caused him much pain, he feels compassion for her in her loneliness. Feeling tremendously guilty for the harm she has caused, she agrees to help Herbert and asks if she can do anything for him (Pip). Pip thanks her but tells her that he is fine. She gives him a note that authorizes Jaggers to give Pip money for Herbert, and then hands him a pad and asks him to at some point, if he can ever forgive her, write down "I forgive her." Unwilling to judge her and filled with shame over his own mistakes, Pip responds that he can do it now. Miss Havisham drops to her knees crying out "What have I done!" She admits that Pip pointed out her mistake, and that her only intent when she adopted Estella was to save her from the same hurts. She now realizes she stole the girl's heart and put ice in its place. Pip asks Miss Havisham if she knows who Estella's mother was, but she only knows that Jaggers brought the girl to her. Before he leaves, Pip walks around the grounds and the brewery where as a child he had the vision of Miss Havisham hanging from the beam. Uncomfortable with the memory, Pip goes back upstairs to check on her and discovers her dress has caught on fire. He saves her from the fire, but his arms are badly burned and she is seriously hurt herself. Through the night the woman mutters over and over in the same order: "What have I done! When she first came, I meant to save her from misery like mine. Take the pencil and write under my name, I forgive her!"

Pip returns to the Temple, and Herbert cares for his wounds. Herbert tells Pip how much Magwitch has "improved," and about Magwitch's wife. When Herbert relates that she killed another woman and their child in a jealous rage, Pip tells Herbert that Magwitch must be Estella's father. Herbert added that Magwitch went into hiding to avoid having to testify against her at her trial. Compeyson blackmailed Magwitch with this information, getting him deeper into crime.

Pip visits Jaggers the next day and is received with more kindness than is usually seen in the office. After resolving the issue of money for Herbert, Pip tells them he knows who Estella's parents are and proceeds to state his findings. Jaggers is surprised but recovers quickly and tries to change the subject back to business. Pip will not be put off this time and indicating his knowledge of Wemmick's emotional side, appeals to both Jaggers and Wemmick to tell him the truth. Jaggers is surprised to hear about the Aged and Wemmick's playful ways, and Wemmick points out that Jaggers is an imposter where emotions are concerned. Jaggers, acknowledging his own former "poor dreams," relents, but agrees to only tell a "theoretical" story.

He tells of a woman in need of legal help who confides in her attorney that her child is really alive, the father does not know this, and that she is guilty of the crime. The attorney, charged with finding a girl to adopt for a rich woman, and knowing the horrors of what happens to children in the legal system, places the child with the rich woman. Here is one child saved regardless of what happens to the mother. The lawyer does his best and saves the woman, but the emotions of it all affect her mind. She is unable to cope with the world. The lawyer takes the theoretical woman in and continues to keep her in line with his power whenever the old, wild ways come out. Stopping, Jaggers then asks Pip if anyone will benefit from knowing this theoretical story. Pip agrees to keep the secret. The episode has upset the unemotional balance between Wemmick and Jaggers who now view each other uncomfortably. The status quo is restored shortly when both of the men rage at a whiny client and tell him that no emotions are allowed in the office.

Commentary

Miss Havisham is suffering, the victim of her lifetime of hatred and vengeance. She has grown through pain to remorse and now desires to make amends. She willingly helps Herbert and offers as much to Pip. The fantasy element about her hanging from the beam is resolved here. Pip, thinking back to that image, goes back inside in time to rescue her from the flames.

Pip is showing reversals here too. He not only refuses any more of Magwitch's money, but he refuses any aid from Miss Havisham. Whatever happens now will be of his own making, a sure sign of growth. He has completed his efforts for Herbert, the only good thing he feels he has done with his money, and gives Miss Havisham the forgiveness she craves. He can do this having seen the hurts he has caused through his own sins in life. He is more in charge of his life now, standing up to Miss Havisham and speaking his mind. His love for Estella is more real and unselfish—he tries to stop her marriage to Drummle by telling her he can bear her marrying anybody else as long as the man loves her. He also displays emotional honesty and passion when demanding the full story of Estella's life from Jaggers and Wemmick. Pip and Herbert have both grown out of some of their snobbery when they notice that Magwitch has "changed and softened." It is actually their perspective on the man that has changed.

There is a moment of truth in Jaggers' office when Pip begs for the whole story of Estella. When Pip speaks of his poor dreams of love that are now dashed, Jaggers responds in a way that shows he once knew this feeling as well. Wemmick, whose emotional side has surprised Jaggers, boldly calls his boss an emotional imposter and suggests that his boss would like a nice home life, too. Jaggers' theoretical story to Pip reveals that he is a deeply caring man who did his best to save a mother and child. However, this level of emotional intensity brings an unstable atmosphere in the law office—both men are relieved to return to the status quo when they scream at a whiny client to bring no emotions to their office. Both men are upset with Pip for passing up Miss Havisham's offer of financial assistance (portable property). They are both realists and genuinely care about Pip's future. Jaggers, the man who knows everyone's secrets, is for one rare moment thrown off guard when Pip tells him Magwitch is Estella's father. It is a secret even he did not know.

Glossary

ivory tablets   a small notebook with two covers made from oblong pieces of ivory. Pencil marks could be wiped off of the ivory.

Chapters 52–54 (Volume III, Chapters 13–15)

Summary

A number of story lines are drawing to a close: Pip completes the transaction with Clarriker for Herbert's business, Herbert will be leaving soon for Egypt, and Pip's life as a wealthy man is over. It is also time to get Magwitch out of England. Receiving a note from Wemmick, they are to make their move Wednesday. Startop, Pip's friend from Mr. Pocket's house, is included because Pip still cannot row due to his burns and Startop is a loyal friend. The plan is to leave early Wednesday and row downriver to pick up Magwitch. They will continue past the Custom's House to Kent and stay at an inn there overnight. Thursday morning they will meet an ocean-going steamer on the river and get Pip and Magwitch aboard. Herbert leaves to get departure schedules for the various steamers, while Pip gets passports.

While Herbert visits Magwitch to tell him the plan, Pip returns home to find a note asking him to come alone, that night or the next, to the sluice-house on the marshes, for important information about his Uncle Provis. Because of the mention of Provis, Pip decides he must go and barely catches the afternoon coach home. He ponders the wisdom of his decision, but feels he must see it through for Magwitch's safety. He orders dinner at a small inn and checks on Miss Havisham while waiting. During dinner the innkeeper tells him about Pumblechook helping some young man become wealthy. Filled with guilt and remorse Pip cannot eat, as the story only strengthens the contrast between Pumblechook's arrogance and Joe and Biddy's true friendship. As it is close to nine, he heads for the marshes and the sluice-house. The flats are abandoned and lonely but there is a light in the sluice-house. He sees no one, but is caught from behind and tied to a ladder inside. His captor is a drunken Orlick, who intends to kill him and put his body in the limekiln so no one will ever find him. As he toys with Pip's nerves, Orlick confesses to killing Mrs. Joe and hiding on the stairs at Pip's London flat. He is now working with someone who knows all about Magwitch and is very powerful. Pip guesses it is Compeyson. Orlick waves the same gun with the brass-bound stock that he had at

Miss Havisham's. Orlick reminds Pip that Pip cost him that job and Biddy, as well. Pip's life flashes before him and Pip realizes he will never have the chance to apologize to Joe and Biddy. He looks for a way to escape but sees none. At the last minute, Pip is rescued by Herbert, Startop, and Trabb's boy. Orlick escapes. Herbert explains that they had found the note to Pip from Orlick so they rushed to Kent. Unable to find him, they encountered Trabb's boy, who served as their guide.

Rushing back to London, they prepare for Wednesday's departure. On Wednesday, all goes well until that night, when they feel they are being followed. The next day, the group heads into the river just as a steamer approaches, but they are intercepted by a boat of customs' agents. They arrest Magwitch, and one of the sitters in the boat turns out to be Compeyson. Unaware of the approaching steamer that is about to run them over, the two convicts struggle and one of the boats capsizes. In a matter of moments Compeyson is drowned and a seriously injured Magwitch is pulled on board the galley. The steamer heads out to sea taking all hope of escape with it.

Herbert and Startop return to London while Pip stays with Magwitch. Any repugnance Pip felt for the man is gone now and he realizes that Magwitch has been a better man to him than Pip has been to Joe. Magwitch wants Pip to leave and save himself, but Pip vows to stay by his side. Pip realizes now why Wemmick wanted him to hold the wallet—with Magwitch arrested, all of the money will be forfeited to the crown. Pip decides there is no need for Magwitch to ever know the truth about that.

Commentary

Pip now shows a great deal of personal growth and caring. He, Herbert, and Startop risk their lives to help Magwitch, and Pip's trip to the marshes, while not smart, was motivated by a concern for Magwitch's safety. He stays by the convict after they are caught instead of trying to "separate himself" from the stain of the criminal element, which used to disturb him so much before. Pip is also seeing reality, recognizing Magwitch's decency and his own failings. Pip also knows the money is gone and he will have to face the reality of survival soon. However, he keeps this from the seriously ill Magwitch, preferring instead to let the convict die with his dream. Pip's guilt is strong when the innkeeper tells him about Pumblechook's bragging, which seems all the worse when compared with Joe's honor.

Magwitch's calmness during the escape is worth noting. He foreshadows the danger and the outcome when he speaks of not being able to see to the end of the next few hours any more than he can see the bottom of the river. Plagued by danger all his life, he has a healthy respect for it and is not afraid to confront it. However, he maintains his calm, feeling he will deal with danger if it comes and not before. Magwitch is softened in Pip's eyes—mostly a change in Pip's perceptions, but also because the convict has had a chance to do something in life that turned out well. He was given a chance to redeem himself and he has. Happy to have seen his gentleman, he is at peace now, however his life turns out. His struggle is over.

Glossary

land of Arabian nights Egypt.

limekiln a furnace or kiln used to turn limestone into lime. Though Dickens places this near the sluice-house, it is unlikely a limekiln could have burned so close to water. It most likely was further inland.

weazen an obsolete word for weasand, meaning throat.

plummet something heavy.

coal-whippers men who operated the whips or pulleys that raised coal onboard ships.

hempen hawsers rope cables.

bowsprit a large, tapered spar extending forward from the bow of a sailing vessel, to which stays for the masts are secured.

capstan an apparatus around which cables or hawsers are wound for hoisting anchors, lifting weights, and so on.

gunwale the upper edge of the side of a ship or boat.

lightermen bargemen.

fenders material, such as timber or old cables, hung over the side of a ship to protect it from banging around while in port.

thowel primitive sort of rowlock or oarlock.

Chapters 55–57
(Volume III, Chapters 16–18)

Summary

Compeyson was supposed to identify Magwitch for the authorities, but because he drowned, the prosecution is delayed three days while they send for one of the old guards from the Hulks to identify him. Jaggers is angry with Pip for letting the money slip through his fingers and says they will try for some of it, though there is little hope of success. Herbert finds out he must leave for Cairo immediately and while Pip is happy for his friend, he fears for his own future. Herbert offers him a job with his firm but Pip delays his answer. For now, he must take care of Magwitch and one other unfinished piece of business.

Wemmick, in his "personal capacity" even though in London, comes by to apologize to Pip for the bad timing of the escape. He also comments on his severe upset over the loss of so much portable property. Pip tells him his concern is for the owner of that property, but Wemmick points out that there probably never was a chance to save Magwitch. Fearing Magwitch, Compeyson had been watching him even in Australia and had hoped to gain some of Magwitch's money as a reward for betraying him. During the conversation, Wemmick tells Pip he is taking a rare holiday on Monday and asks Pip to oblige him this once with his presence. Out of gratitude for all his help, Pip agrees.

When Pip arrives, Wemmick carries a fishing pole and pretends they are going for a walk. Their walk just happens to end at a church where everything is ready for a wedding, and he just happens to have a ring. Pip serves his friend as best man in his marriage to Miss Skiffins. Later, as Pip leaves, Wemmick reminds him that this is completely a Walworth sentiment, not to be mentioned in Little Britain because Jaggers may think Wemmick's brain is softening.

Pip spends all his time with Magwitch, who continues to worsen. Magwitch reflects on whether he might have lived a better life under better circumstances, but he makes no excuses. His trial is quick and he is condemned to die. Magwitch thanks Pip for his steadfastness in visiting and notes that Pip is more comfortable with him now that he is in trouble than when he was free. As Magwitch dies, Pip whispers to him that his daughter whom he thought was dead, is, in fact, alive and a lady, and that Pip loves her. Magwitch smiles and dies in peace. Pip's problems worsen as he is in debt and quite ill. Men come to arrest him for a debt but Pip is so ill he cannot be moved. He falls into a delirious state and imagines that Joe is there with him. When he finally he comes out of the fever he realizes Joe has been there all along, urged by Biddy to go to him right away. Pip is overwhelmed and asks Joe to be angry with him or hit him, just not to be good to him.

While there Pip sees that Joe has learned to write—Biddy taught him—and hears that Miss Havisham has died, leaving a "cool four thousand" to Matthew Pocket because of Pip's account of him. He also learns that Orlick was arrested after breaking into Pumblechook's house. Pip tries to tell Joe about Magwitch, intending to tell him the whole truth. Joe cuts him off, instead speaking to his own failings at protecting Pip when he (Pip) was a boy. When Pip says Joe was not wrong, Joe tells him that, regarding the convict, they have nothing to discuss, either. Joe nurses him to health and loves him unconditionally but as Pip recovers Joe pulls back and resumes calling him "Sir." Pip is upset but realizes Joe does not know it is different this time. Intending to level with Joe about his debts, his guilt over treating Joe so badly, and his interest in asking Biddy to marry him, Pip gets up early the next day to find Joe already gone. There is a receipt showing Joe paid off Pip's debt. A couple days later, Pip heads home to talk to Joe and Biddy.

Commentary

Pip has softened much himself by this point in the novel. He has given up his snobbish attempt to distance himself from the criminal stain and is genuinely caring to Magwitch, whom Pip has come to realize is a better man than he is. He does this from his heart, not for financial gain, and even Magwitch notices that Pip is more comfortable with him now as a condemned man than as a free one. Some literary analysts feel that Pip felt free to love Magwitch only because he knew the man was dying and that if Magwitch lived, Pip would not have been able to sustain that emotion. However, Pip's concern appears genuine and he does offer great comfort to the dying man by staying by his side. Abandoned his whole life, Magwitch treasures Pip's loyalty as he dies.

Pip is overwhelmed with emotion during his own illness. After everything Pip has done to hurt them both, Joe has come to nurse him and Biddy sent him. Joe and Pip are able to talk about some long-standing issues between them, such as Joe's guilt over not protecting Pip more as a child, and Pip's guilt over lying to him about the convict on the marshes. Joe makes it all a non-issue when he points out that if Pip forgives his failure, he sees no failure on Pip's part. Maybe a more full and open discussion would have been a better choice, but Joe waves away people's failures and focuses on the present. Joe also points out that Pip's good word to Miss Havisham got Matthew Pocket a lot of money.

Character Insight

There is also a change in Joe, who has learned to write and takes pride in it. In the past, he avoided learning but has come to accept it as a good idea. Pip was never wrong in wanting Joe to learn—education is not a bad thing— but Pip was wrong in *why* he wanted Joe to learn. As Pip gets better, Joe assumes that the old snobbish status quo will return, so he leaves. This time, though, things are different. Pip is different. Not only does he have an honorable *intention*, he follows it with an honorable *action* and he does it *in person*, not long distance or through another. He goes home to make amends with Joe and to ask Biddy to marry him.

Dickens infuses some humor as he ties up loose ends. Wemmick's wedding is a classic piece because of Wemmick's acting as if the whole thing is a surprise. Wemmick's compliment for his bride that she is such a manager of fowls is humorously unromantic but full of love and admiration and very characteristic of Wemmick. Miss Havisham's leaving Sarah Pocket enough money for pills for being bilious, and Camilla enough to buy lights for when she sits up at night "worrying" about everyone, humorously answers what happens to the toady relatives. Even Orlick's arrest has its humor when Dickens makes fun of Pumblechook one last time: "they took his till, and they took his cash-box, and they drinked his wine, and they partook of his wittles . . . and they stuffed his mouth full of flowering annuals." This is probably the only time in the whole book that Pumblechook is quiet.

Glossary

Hymen the Greek god of marriage, the son of Dionysus and Aphrodite.

bagatelle board a slanted oblong table that was raised at one end and used to play a nineteenth century version of pinball with a wooden ball, a wooden cue, and numbered holes.

nosegays small bouquets of flowers, such as for carrying in the hand.

gewgaws things that are showy but useless; trinkets.

two men up into the Temple to pray reference to the biblical parable from Luke 18:10-13, in which a Pharisee and a publican go into the temple to pray. The Pharisee is proud, while the publican is humble and asks God to forgive him because he is a sinner. Pip is thinking of these verses as he stands at Magwitch's deathbed. Magwitch has just died, and Pip concludes that the best prayer he can make is "Oh Lord, be merciful to him, a sinner!"

Chapters 58–59
(Volume III, Chapters 19–20)

Summary

On his return home, Pip meets Pumblechook who magnanimously "forgives" Pip for his ingratitude, and Joe, for his stupidity. Pip acidly tells the man that his benefactor is not in the room. Walking toward the forge, Pip is worried because it is closed. He is then overwhelmed to find out Joe and Biddy have just been married. Pip is relieved he never told Joe that he himself had wanted to propose to Biddy. Joe and Biddy are thrilled to see him. Pip apologizes to them and tells them he is going to join Herbert in Egypt. He promises to repay them and asks that they remember him kindly.

In Egypt, Pip lives with Herbert and Clara, pays off his debts, and leads a frugal life. He honors his promise to pay Joe back and writes frequent letters to Joe and Biddy. Pip eventually becomes a third partner in the firm, at which point Clarriker tells Herbert how Pip secretly got him started in the business. Pip acknowledges to himself that the firm's success is due in large part to Herbert's talents, and he realizes his initial assessment of Herbert as inept was more likely the ineptness in himself. Eleven years later, Pip returns to the forge to visit Joe, Biddy, their daughter, and young son, Pip. He offers to borrow Pip but Biddy gently tells him he must marry. Pip acknowledges that even Herbert and Clara tell him this, but he indicates he is an old bachelor and content in his ways. Biddy asks if he still longs for Estella.

Before nightfall, Pip walks to the site of Satis House, and wandering the grounds, comes across a solitary figure in the shadows—Estella. She has changed, time and trouble softening the proud eyes. Estella tells Pip that she has thought of him much lately, though for a long time she could not because it hurt to think of what she threw away. They rise to part and Estella asks if he will think of her as a friend. Pip tells her they are friends and observes to himself that he saw "the shadow of no parting from her."

Commentary

Pip has finally accepted responsibility for his sins, debts, and life. He is frugal, remembers to write Joe and Biddy, and pays his debts. His maturity is evident when, instead of being upset that Joe beat him to marrying Biddy, he feels relief that he never mentioned his own wish to do the same. He also looks at others in a new light, acknowledging that the firm's success is due to Herbert's talents and that his original opinion of Herbert's ineptness was really his own ineptness showing.

The secret of Pip setting Herbert up in business is revealed, leaving only one secret left at the end of the story that Pip holds in his heart—Estella's parentage. Dickens never does say whether the final secret of Estella's parentage is ever revealed. Most likely, Pip takes it to his grave. Dickens provided two endings to this story. The original ending had Estella remarried to a Shropshire doctor, meeting Pip once in London and exchanging pleasantries, and then each going their separate ways. Dickens' own life had a precedent for this when he met his first love, Maria Beadnell, many years later in his life. By then she was very fat and his image of her was crushed. Certainly here Dickens has Estella losing some of her beauty and wearied a bit by life. But overall he treats Estella kindly. Dickens, instead, took the advice of a novelist friend and changed the ending to give Pip, Estella, and the readers a chance for a happy conclusion. However, the ending is ambiguous and no one is certain if the "shadow of no parting" means they stay together or not.

CHARACTER ANALYSES

The following character analyses delve into the physical, emotional, and psychological traits of the literary work's major characters so that you might better understand what motivates these characters. The writer of this study guide provides this scholarship as an educational tool by which you may compare your own interpretations of the characters. Before reading the character analyses that follow, consider first writing your own short essays on the characters as an exercise by which you can test your understanding of the original literary work. Then, compare your essays to those that follow, noting discrepancies between the two. If your essays appear lacking, that might indicate that you need to re-read the original literary work or re-familiarize yourself with the major characters.

Pip

Pip has low self-esteem. He is not valued and does not value himself. He feels guilty for his very existence, thanks to his sister who constantly reminds him how she has suffered because of him. Other relatives and friends reinforce his feelings by telling him how grateful he should be. His only positive in life is Joe, and Pip looks forward to being his apprentice in the forge. Miss Havisham and Estella, however, destroy that dream when they teach him to be ashamed of his coarse and common life. Their influence, coupled with his low self-worth and his sister's messages about wealth and security, fuel his desires, ambitions, and snobbery.

Pip, abused by his sister, is a passive personality who fears the stronger emotions in him. He rarely shows power, passion, or self-determination, reacting instead to those around him and living his life as a dreamer. The fantasy world of Satis House feeds that part of him. Shut from the light of day, Miss Havisham lives in her strange world. Pip responds to this and preserves that world by keeping the light of day—questions his sister and Pumblechook ask—from destroying its special fairy-tale quality. That world is something that is his, and it holds his only passion in life, the fairy-tale princess he desires, Estella. In that world there are things he has never seen—beauty, wealth, polish, power—and they dazzle him. They become his quest in life and he will give up everything—Joe, the forge, his own good conscience and behavior—to get money and Estella.

In Pip, the reader sees several of the themes of the novel: obsession, desire, greed, guilt, ambition, wealth, and good and evil. Pip leaves his state of childish innocence and "grace" and descends into sin on his quest to gain his desires. He wants it all and he wants no costs. Yet Dickens does not make him totally bad, instead leaving the truly good qualities asleep underneath. They surface as his guilt over his snobbery to Joe and Biddy, over dragging Herbert into debt, and about trading Joe for a convict's money. Even during his worst moments, Pip manages to show some good, as, for example, when he sets Herbert up in business. His road back to grace starts when Magwitch reveals himself as the source of Pip's rise in social stature. The irony that the source of his gentility is from a creature more socially detestable than the uneducated Joe is not lost on Pip. It is the slap in the face that brings Pip out of the fantasy world he has been living in. His dream has suddenly been seen in the light of day, and now he knows what it has cost him.

The concepts of self-responsibility and the cost for choices make up his lessons in the last part of the book. Nothing in life comes free and one must accept the consequences of the choices made. Dickens generously gives Pip four "father figures" in the book to model this for him. Joe makes his choice to stay with Mrs. Joe and show her more love than his mother had, fully accepting the cost of enduring her abuse. Jaggers chooses control and an emotionless life and accepts the cost of loneliness and alienation. Wemmick knows the only way to support himself, his father, and their home is to endure an emotionless job that could drive him crazy if he let it; he accepts responsibility by keeping his work and home life separate and knowingly accepts and pays the price for his actions. Magwitch knows the cost for seeing his "dear boy" is death, makes his choice to go to England anyway, and accepts the outcome. Pip learns from all of them that there are no free rides, that wealth does not guarantee freedom from consequences, and in the end he has to take responsibility for whatever he chooses.

Joe Gargery

He is the closest thing in the story to a totally good character. Hard working, honorable, loyal, and fair, he is equally comfortable showing both his raw, physical strength and his gentle, patient, emotional side. He is compassionate to the convict who stole his food, as well as to the memory of his alcoholic, abusive father. He recognizes Mrs. Joe's strengths, remembers her better times, and wants to protect her from the suffering that his mother endured with his father. In him, there is deep intuitive wisdom, inner peace and acceptance, dignity, and a basic sense of what is right and what will cause heartache. Even when treated poorly by Pip, he shows unconditional love and comes to Pip's aid when needed. His function in the story is to love Pip, be a father to him, and show him the path to dignified manhood.

Dickens keeps him from being a sickeningly sweet person by giving him the flaws of no education, no polish, and failing to better protect Pip from his sister when Pip was a child. Yet, to his credit, Joe himself expresses his realization of that and does what he exemplifies best. He takes responsibility for himself and consciously chooses his actions. He is not ruled by passion or illusion.

Magwitch

Magwitch, as a young man, is what Joe would have been if Joe had been ruled by his passions and reacted to life instead of taking responsibility for his choices. Magwitch is another father figure for Pip, showing both what happens with bad choices and how you can rise above them. During his rough childhood, he kept reacting to life, getting into ever worsening criminal activities. Yet removed from England and placed in a new environment where he is given the chance to become what he was always capable of, he rises to the occasion. The hidden good has a chance to come out. He remembers the generosity of a small boy, feeling the bond of powerlessness and victimization they both shared as convict and child. He recommits his life, this time a conscious choice, to do good. He works hard, so that Pip can live easy.

His flaw is in wanting to return to see and show off his creation. His generosity is great, but it is not perfect and not done just for Pip's benefit. Magwitch wants revenge on society and uses Pip to do it. He wants to create a wonderful gentleman to show society they were wrong about him. He wants to feel proud of what he created. This is his downfall because to return and glory in this is to risk his life. However, he is a true man and accepts that risk knowingly, never playing the victim. He wants to see Pip, will pay with his life if he has to, and is at peace with that. He loves Pip with a simple heart, and, having had a chance to return to the basic tenderness that was always within him, dies with dignity and peace.

Mrs. Joe

Abusive and self-important, Mrs. Joe appears to be total evil; however, some of her behavior is understandable. When she was twenty, before this story begins, she was left alone with a helpless infant brother who was not even weaned. By the time the reader is introduced to her, she has already buried two parents and five brothers and has no husband, and hence, no means to support herself. Joe solves that by marrying her. However, because of all the loss in her life early on, she fears abandonment and wants security, so her focus is survival. She seeks it through power and wealth and unconsciously communicates these values to Pip. Joe alludes to her fear of abandonment when he notes that she does not want Joe to better himself. That would take away her power in handling the business end of things in their relationship, and may even give Joe the opportunity to leave her.

Miss Havisham

She is one of the most strange and grotesque characters in the story, the "wicked witch" of the fairy tale. In adopting Estella, she seeks to protect the girl from the hurts she herself has suffered. That intention, however, degrades into her training Estella to love no one and exact revenge from all men. Miss Havisham was proud, beautiful, passionate, and headstrong, things Compeyson used against her. Deeply hurt, reeling from the loss of control she felt by the betrayal, and determined to regain both control and self-image, Miss Havisham chooses her lifestyle. She wields her money as her weapon of power and trains her daughter to succeed where she has failed. But it backfires. Estella ends up not only unable to love men, but unable to love Miss Havisham. Miss Havisham's creation is her downfall, and Pip is her mirror. When she sees the depth of Pip's feelings for Estella, Miss Havisham sees herself with Compeyson and remembers what she once was. Her redemption is in seeing her sins and showing her remorse. She does the only thing she can do—takes responsibility for her actions. She asks Pip's forgiveness, helps Herbert Pocket, and leaves a fortune to Herbert's father.

Estella

Like Pip, Estella is an orphan and a victim. Both had surrogate mothers who thought they were doing the right things. Both are used by their surrogate parents—Estella by Miss Havisham and Pip by Magwitch—to extract revenge from society. Both share a somewhat passive approach to life that she alludes to when she says they are both unable to follow their own free path but must do the bidding of another. She is an honest character, not evil, and is what she was trained to be. She cannot love Pip or Miss Havisham because she was not taught love, and she says so quite honestly. There is no manipulation, only frankness. She also shows a sort of loyalty to Pip when she tells him she will toy with all men, but him. There is an acknowledgement that she knows Pip loves her, she cannot love him, and therefore she will not be with a man who will realize she has nothing to give him. Yet underneath this rigid unemotional surface is the passion and emotional fury of her parents, Molly and Magwitch. The one time she responds to Pip and lets him kiss her is when he displays rare aggression and forcefulness in beating the Pale Young Gentleman. There is, deep within her, something that responds to emotional fury. That is the part that is changed and softened by the abuse Drummle hands her in their marriage.

Jaggers and Wemmick

Jaggers and Wemmick are two more father figures who teach Pip how to be a man. Jaggers is a hard-working, self-made man, who is direct, true to fact, and a good man in his own way. Seeing the horrors of prison, and the abuse of children by the legal system, he takes in Molly and finds a home for Estella. But he seeks his security in control and power, and chooses to wash off both emotions and people instead of embracing them. He pays a cost in his life, knows it, and accepts it.

Wemmick is the transition character: a little of Joe and of Jaggers. He is true to fact in the office, and true to emotion at home. With Pip, he risks mixing his two worlds in London, something he would not do before, but he reaffirms the status quo of separation when he savages the client in the office for crying, and when he tells Pip at his wedding that Jaggers should not know of this. Wemmick is pragmatic about "portable property" because he cannot afford to be any other way. He is not rich and has a father and house to support. But he is also caring, industrious, creative, has an emotional side—even gets married. He embraces life, but draws a line to survive in his dual world.

CRITICAL ESSAYS

On the pages that follow, the writer of this study guide provides critical scholarship on various aspects of Dickens' *Great Expectations*. These interpretive essays are intended solely to enhance your understanding of the original literary work; they are supplemental materials and are not to replace your reading of *Great Expectations*. When you're finished reading *Great Expectations*, and prior to your reading this study guide's critical essays, consider making a bulleted list of what you think are the most important themes and symbols. Write a short paragraph under each bullet explaining why you think that theme or symbol is important; include at least one short quote from the original literary work that supports your contention. Then, test your list and reasons against those found in the following essays. Do you include themes and symbols that the study guide author doesn't? If so, this self test might indicate that you are well on your way to understanding original literary work. But if not, perhaps you will need to re-read *Great Expectations*.

The Unusual Case of the Serial Form

To present-day readers, the idea of reading a novel in weekly or monthly installments may seem strange. Why buy twenty issues of a magazine when the paperback costs a few dollars and you get the whole story at once? But as one writer in 1828 noted, "No Englishman in the middle class of life *buys* a book." At that time, one complete novel might be published in three or four volumes at a cost of roughly three to four hundred dollars for a complete novel. Given this, anyone who wanted to read a book and who was not rich joined a lending library or bought the weekly issues of a magazine. Thus novels, once only the domain of the rich, became a cheap luxury for the masses.

This method of publishing affected how the novels were actually written. Authors' choices of plot, character, and style were often a direct results of the requirements of publishing in serial form. (In fact, some of the flaws of which Dickens is accused by modern-day reviewers are actually constraints of this form.)

The first consideration in planning a book for this form was the number of installments to use to tell the story. Each installment needed to be about the same length, roughly thirty-two pages of fifty lines per page. The emotional intensity and action had to be about equal in each, as well. After a break in the story of a week or month, the pressing question was: Would the reader come back and buy the next issue? Hence each installment had to be a "mini-story" or "episode" in itself, each with its own cliffhanger ending. To achieve so many cliffhangers, plots had to be large and complex with a lot of action.

The same applied to the story's characters. They were often odd and given unusual and sometimes almost "excessive" characteristics so the readers could remember them from week-to-week or month-to-month. In *Great Expectations*, Dickens used character tags, such as Jaggers biting his finger or Wemmick having a "post-office mouth." While these traits or tags were a necessity because of this fragmented publishing method, this much repetition in a story published as a solid book can drive the reader crazy.

The writing for serials had to be rapid because of tight deadlines. Often the author was still plotting action or figuring out the ending as he went along, and half the book had already been published. It was a shoot-from-the-hip method in many respects because it also took into account readers' reactions to the story. If something was not working and circulation dropped, the author could change a character's response or add another cliffhanger to beef up the audience's interest. The action also had to be fast because every word counted. Space in the magazines was money. In contrast to a one-thousand-page novel, *Great Expectations*, done in serial form, was considered downright short. The Victorians wanted a lot for their money and they expected a sweeping story with lots of twists and turns. Charles Dickens gave them exactly that and was very successful with his reading public.

Children and Nineteenth-Century England

For thousands of years, families put their children to work on their farms or in whatever labor was necessary for survival—only children of the wealthy and powerful escaped this fate. Until the last one hundred years or so, children were considered by most societies to be the property of their parents. They had little protection from governments who viewed children as having no human or civil rights outside of their parents' wishes, and *Great Expectations* brings some of these conditions to light.

The industrial revolution in early nineteenth-century England (the industrial revolution started about one hundred years later in the United States) made things worse. Laborers were in greater demand than ever. Mines, factories, and shops needed help, and not enough men or women could fill their needs. Children were cheap, plentiful, and easy to control. Orphanages—and even parents—would give their children to the owners of cotton mills and other operations in exchange for the cost of maintaining them.

At that time, the government didn't establish a minimum age, wage, or working hours. Children as young as five or six were forced to work thirteen to sixteen hours a day for slave wages and barely any food. The Sadler Committee, investigating textile factory conditions for Parliament in 1832, discovered children working from six in the morning to nine at night with no breakfast, one hour for lunch, and a two-mile walk home. Children late for work were often beaten, and if they worked too slowly or fell asleep at the machines, they were hit with a strap, sometimes severely. There was no family time and some of them did not get supper because they were too tired to wait for it. Children who were "bound" to companies often tried to run away. If they were caught, they were whipped. Aside from being underfed, exhausted, sick, or injured, children spending so many hours a day over factory machines often had bowed legs and poorly developed limbs and muscles.

The coal mines were worse, with young children having to travel through the mines without any light, often carrying loads while walking in water that was up to their calves. The main reason for employing women and children in the mines was that they would work for less than a man would accept.

If a child was not "lucky" enough to be employed in these manners, they had the unpleasant option of life on the streets, with its raw sewage, rotting animal and vegetable wastes in the streets, rats, disease, and bad water. They also had to find food and a place to stay out of the rain and cold. Turning to crime for survival was not an act of greed so much as one of pure need. Small wonder, then, that Magwitch turned to crime at a young age.

As the century progressed, laws were passed that outlawed infant abandonment and failure to provide shelter, clothing, food, and medical care. In 1884, national laws in Britain protected children in their own homes. In addition, Parliament regulated working conditions, minimum age for working, and the length of the workday for children. Laws for mandatory schooling, however, did not come until the twentieth century.

CliffsNotes Review

Use this CliffsNotes Review to test your understanding of the original text, and reinforce what you've learned in this book. After you work through the essay questions and useful practice projects, you're well on your way to understanding a comprehensive and meaningful interpretation of *Great Expectations*.

Q&A

1. What does it mean to bring someone up "by hand"?

2. What are the two conditions for Pip's expectations?

3. When Pip returns to his London home from a visit to Miss Havisham's, the gatekeeper gives him a note. What does it say and who is it from?

4. At the end of the story Miss Havisham hands Pip a notepad and pencil. What does she want him to write on the pad?

Answers: (1) Bottle-feed instead of nurse a baby. (2) Pip is to keep the name "Pip" and he is not to ask who his benefactor is. (3) "Don't go home." Wemmick. (4) "I forgive her."

Identify the Quote: Find each Quote in *Great Expectations*

1. "Be grateful, boy, to them which brought you up by hand."

2. "And it were my intentions to have had put upon his tombstone that Whatsume'r the failings on his part, Remember reader he were that good in his heart."

3. "If you can't get to be oncommon through going straight, you'll never get to do it through going crooked."

4. "I am as unhappy as you can ever have meant me to be."

5. "Should I fling myself away upon the man who would the soonest feel that I took nothing to him?"

Answers: (1) Pumblechook telling Pip to be grateful to Mrs. Joe. (2) Joe speaking to Pip about what he wanted to put on his father's tombstone.

(3) Joe speaking to Pip, when Pip admits he lied when describing Miss Havisham's house. (4) Pip speaking to Miss Havisham at the end of the novel when he finds out Estella is marrying Drummle. (5) Estelle telling Pip why she is marrying Drummle instead of a better man.

Essay Questions

1. Why does Joe put up with Mrs. Joe's abuse? Do you agree with his choice, and did he do enough to protect Pip?

2. Do you think Miss Havisham was really rewarding Pip with the apprenticeship? Was it actually more revenge on men by chaining him to the forge when he preferred to be with Estella?

3. Why does Pip refuse to take any more of Magwitch's money? Was this the correct choice? Why or why not?

4. Which of the two endings do you prefer? If neither, how would you end the novel?

5. Does Estella's change at the end of the novel seem real?

Practice Projects

1. Keep a weekly log. At the end of each week of reading the text, each student writes down any questions, complaints, insights, or confusions; in short, anything at all they want to note about the story. These can be on index cards and can be anonymous or signed. The cards can then be used for either a class discussion or passed out to class groups for their own discussion.

2. A variation on the previous idea is to use e-mail lists or Web-site chat rooms for comments, thus allowing the discussion to flow freely anytime. Students can also discuss what other features and resources to include on a Web page.

CliffsNotes Resource Center

The learning doesn't need to stop here. CliffsNotes Resource Center shows you the best of the best—links to the best information in print and online about the author and/or related works. And don't think that this is all we've prepared for you; we've put all kinds of pertinent information at www.cliffsnotes.com. Look for all the terrific resources at your favorite bookstore or local library and on the Internet. When you're online, make your first stop www.cliffsnotes.com where you'll find more incredibly useful information about Charles Dickens and *Great Expectations*.

Books

This CliffsNotes book, published by Wiley Publishing, Inc., provides a meaningful interpretation of *Great Expectations*. If you are looking for information about the author and/or related works, check out these other publications:

DICKENS, CHARLES. *Great Expectations*. Ed. Charlotte Mitchell. New York: Penguin Classics-Penguin, 1996.

DICKENS, CHARLES. *Great Expectations*. Ed. Edgar Rosenberg. A Norton Critical Edition. New York: Norton, 1999.

HARRIS, LAURIE LANZEN, ed. *Nineteenth-Century Literature Criticism*. Vol. 3. Detroit: Gale Research, 1983.

KAPLAN, FRED. *Dickens: A Biography*. New York: William Morrow, 1988.

KAPPEL, LAWRENCE, ed. *Readings on Great Expectations*. The Greenhaven Press Literary Companion to British Literature. Ed. Bonnie Szumski. San Diego: Greenhaven Press, 1999.

MULLANE, JANET, and ROBERT THOMAS WILSON, eds. *Nineteenth-Century Literature Criticism*. Vol. 26. Detroit: Gale Research, 1990.

ORWELL, GEORGE. "Charles Dickens." *George Orwell: A Collection of Essays*. New York: Harvest-Harcourt, 1981.

It's easy to find books published by Wiley Publishing, Inc., and other publishers. You'll find them in your favorite bookstores (on the Internet and at a store near you). We also have three Web sites that you can use to read about all the books we publish:

- www.cliffsnotes.com

- www.dummies.com

- www.wiley.com

Films

Great Expectations. Directed by David Lean. John Mills, Jean Simmons, and Alec Guinness. Cineguild, 1946.

Great Expectations. Directed by Alfonso Cuaron. Anne Bancroft, Robert DeNiro, Ethan Hawke, Gwyneth Paltrow. Twentieth Century Fox, 1998.

Internet

Check out these Web resources for more information about Charles Dickens:

Concordances-Dickens, Charles-55 Works, http://www.concordance.com/dickens.html—allows for text and word searches of passages or words from several of Dickens' works.

The Dickens Project, http://humwww.ucsc.edu/dickens/index.html—gives superb information on electronic links, online discussion groups, teaching guides and publications, and the latest discussions on Dickens' works.

Next time you're on the Internet, don't forget to drop by www.cliffsnotes.com. We've created an online Resource Center that you can use today, tomorrow, and beyond.

Index

CliffsNotes

LITERATURE NOTES

Absalom, Absalom!
The Aeneid
Agamemnon
Alice in Wonderland
All the King's Men
All the Pretty Horses
All Quiet on the
    Western Front
All's Well &
    Merry Wives
American Poets of the
    20th Century
American Tragedy
Animal Farm
Anna Karenina
Anthem
Antony and Cleopatra
Aristotle's Ethics
As I Lay Dying
The Assistant
As You Like It
Atlas Shrugged
Autobiography of
    Ben Franklin
Autobiography of
    Malcolm X
The Awakening
Babbit
Bartleby & Benito
    Cereno
The Bean Trees
The Bear
The Bell Jar
Beloved
Beowulf
The Bible
Billy Budd & Typee
Black Boy
Black Like Me
Bleak House
Bless Me, Ultima
The Bluest Eye & Sula
Brave New World
Brothers Karamazov

The Call of the Wild &
    White Fang
Candide
The Canterbury Tales
Catch-22
Catcher in the Rye
The Chosen
The Color Purple
Comedy of Errors…
Connecticut Yankee
The Contender
The Count of
    Monte Cristo
Crime and Punishment
The Crucible
Cry, the Beloved
    Country
Cyrano de Bergerac
Daisy Miller &
    Turn…Screw
David Copperfield
Death of a Salesman
The Deerslayer
Diary of Anne Frank
Divine Comedy-I.
    Inferno
Divine Comedy-II.
    Purgatorio
Divine Comedy-III.
    Paradiso
Doctor Faustus
Dr. Jekyll and Mr. Hyde
Don Juan
Don Quixote
Dracula
Electra & Medea
Emerson's Essays
Emily Dickinson Poems
Emma
Ethan Frome
The Faerie Queene
Fahrenheit 451
Far from the Madding
    Crowd
A Farewell to Arms
Farewell to Manzanar
Fathers and Sons
Faulkner's Short Stories

Faust Pt. I & Pt. II
The Federalist
Flowers for Algernon
For Whom the Bell Tolls
The Fountainhead
Frankenstein
The French
    Lieutenant's Woman
The Giver
Glass Menagerie &
    Streetcar
Go Down, Moses
The Good Earth
The Grapes of Wrath
Great Expectations
The Great Gatsby
Greek Classics
Gulliver's Travels
Hamlet
The Handmaid's Tale
Hard Times
Heart of Darkness &
    Secret Sharer
Hemingway's
    Short Stories
Henry IV Part 1
Henry IV Part 2
Henry V
House Made of Dawn
The House of the
    Seven Gables
Huckleberry Finn
I Know Why the
    Caged Bird Sings
Ibsen's Plays I
Ibsen's Plays II
The Idiot
Idylls of the King
The Iliad
Incidents in the Life of
    a Slave Girl
Inherit the Wind
Invisible Man
Ivanhoe
Jane Eyre
Joseph Andrews
The Joy Luck Club
Jude the Obscure

Julius Caesar
The Jungle
Kafka's Short Stories
Keats & Shelley
The Killer Angels
King Lear
The Kitchen God's Wife
The Last of the
    Mohicans
Le Morte d'Arthur
Leaves of Grass
Les Miserables
A Lesson Before Dying
Light in August
The Light in the Forest
Lord Jim
Lord of the Flies
The Lord of the Rings
Lost Horizon
Lysistrata & Other
    Comedies
Macbeth
Madame Bovary
Main Street
The Mayor of
    Casterbridge
Measure for Measure
The Merchant
    of Venice
Middlemarch
A Midsummer Night's
    Dream
The Mill on the Floss
Moby-Dick
Moll Flanders
Mrs. Dalloway
Much Ado About
    Nothing
My Ántonia
Mythology
Narr. …Frederick
    Douglass
Native Son
New Testament
Night
1984
Notes from the
    Underground

CliffsNotes™
@ cliffsnotes.com

Check Out the All-New CliffsNotes Guides

TECHNOLOGY TOPICS

PERSONAL FINANCE TOPICS

CAREER TOPICS